Mometrix TEST PREPARATION

AP®

Macroeconomics Exam Secrets Study Guide

DEAR FUTURE EXAM SUCCESS STORY

First of all, **THANK YOU** for purchasing Mometrix study materials!

Second, congratulations! You are one of the few determined test-takers who are committed to doing whatever it takes to excel on your exam. **You have come to the right place.** We developed these study materials with one goal in mind: to deliver you the information you need in a format that's concise and easy to use.

In addition to optimizing your guide for the content of the test, we've outlined our recommended steps for breaking down the preparation process into small, attainable goals so you can make sure you stay on track.

We've also analyzed the entire test-taking process, identifying the most common pitfalls and showing how you can overcome them and be ready for any curveball the test throws you.

Standardized testing is one of the biggest obstacles on your road to success, which only increases the importance of doing well in the high-pressure, high-stakes environment of test day. Your results on this test could have a significant impact on your future, and this guide provides the information and practical advice to help you achieve your full potential on test day.

Your success is our success

We would love to hear from you! If you would like to share the story of your exam success or if you have any questions or comments in regard to our products, please contact us at **800-673-8175** or **support@mometrix.com**.

Thanks again for your business and we wish you continued success!

Sincerely,
The Mometrix Test Preparation Team

Need more help? Check out our flashcards at:
http://MometrixFlashcards.com/AP

Table of Contents

Introduction

Thank you for purchasing this resource! You have made the choice to prepare yourself for a test that could have a huge impact on your future, and this guide is designed to help you be fully ready for test day. Obviously, it's important to have a solid understanding of the test material, but you also need to be prepared for the unique environment and stressors of the test, so that you can perform to the best of your abilities.

For this purpose, the first section that appears in this guide is the **Secret Keys**. We've devoted countless hours to meticulously researching what works and what doesn't, and we've boiled down our findings to the five most impactful steps you can take to improve your performance on the test. We start at the beginning with study planning and move through the preparation process, all the way to the testing strategies that will help you get the most out of what you know when you're finally sitting in front of the test.

We recommend that you start preparing for your test as far in advance as possible. However, if you've bought this guide as a last-minute study resource and only have a few days before your test, we recommend that you skip over the first two Secret Keys since they address a long-term study plan.

If you struggle with **test anxiety**, we strongly encourage you to check out our recommendations for how you can overcome it. Test anxiety is a formidable foe, but it can be beaten, and we want to make sure you have the tools you need to defeat it.

Secret Key #1 – Plan Big, Study Small

There's a lot riding on your performance. If you want to ace this test, you're going to need to keep your skills sharp and the material fresh in your mind. You need a plan that lets you review everything you need to know while still fitting in your schedule. We'll break this strategy down into three categories.

Information Organization

Start with the information you already have: the official test outline. From this, you can make a complete list of all the concepts you need to cover before the test. Organize these concepts into groups that can be studied together, and create a list of any related vocabulary you need to learn so you can brush up on any difficult terms. You'll want to keep this vocabulary list handy once you actually start studying since you may need to add to it along the way.

Time Management

Once you have your set of study concepts, decide how to spread them out over the time you have left before the test. Break your study plan into small, clear goals so you have a manageable task for each day and know exactly what you're doing. Then just focus on one small step at a time. When you manage your time this way, you don't need to spend hours at a time studying. Studying a small block of content for a short period each day helps you retain information better and avoid stressing over how much you have left to do. You can relax knowing that you have a plan to cover everything in time. In order for this strategy to be effective though, you have to start studying early and stick to your schedule. Avoid the exhaustion and futility that comes from last-minute cramming!

Study Environment

The environment you study in has a big impact on your learning. Studying in a coffee shop, while probably more enjoyable, is not likely to be as fruitful as studying in a quiet room. It's important to keep distractions to a minimum. You're only planning to study for a short block of time, so make the most of it. Don't pause to check your phone or get up to find a snack. It's also important to **avoid multitasking**. Research has consistently shown that multitasking will make your studying dramatically less effective. Your study area should also be comfortable and well-lit so you don't have the distraction of straining your eyes or sitting on an uncomfortable chair.

The time of day you study is also important. You want to be rested and alert. Don't wait until just before bedtime. Study when you'll be most likely to comprehend and remember. Even better, if you know what time of day your test will be, set that time aside for study. That way your brain will be used to working on that subject at that specific time and you'll have a better chance of recalling information.

Finally, it can be helpful to team up with others who are studying for the same test. Your actual studying should be done in as isolated an environment as possible, but the work of organizing the information and setting up the study plan can be divided up. In between study sessions, you can discuss with your teammates the concepts that you're all studying and quiz each other on the details. Just be sure that your teammates are as serious about the test as you are. If you find that your study time is being replaced with social time, you might need to find a new team.

Secret Key #2 – Make Your Studying Count

You're devoting a lot of time and effort to preparing for this test, so you want to be absolutely certain it will pay off. This means doing more than just reading the content and hoping you can remember it on test day. It's important to make every minute of study count. There are two main areas you can focus on to make your studying count.

Retention

It doesn't matter how much time you study if you can't remember the material. You need to make sure you are retaining the concepts. To check your retention of the information you're learning, try recalling it at later times with minimal prompting. Try carrying around flashcards and glance at one or two from time to time or ask a friend who's also studying for the test to quiz you.

To enhance your retention, look for ways to put the information into practice so that you can apply it rather than simply recalling it. If you're using the information in practical ways, it will be much easier to remember. Similarly, it helps to solidify a concept in your mind if you're not only reading it to yourself but also explaining it to someone else. Ask a friend to let you teach them about a concept you're a little shaky on (or speak aloud to an imaginary audience if necessary). As you try to summarize, define, give examples, and answer your friend's questions, you'll understand the concepts better and they will stay with you longer. Finally, step back for a big picture view and ask yourself how each piece of information fits with the whole subject. When you link the different concepts together and see them working together as a whole, it's easier to remember the individual components.

Finally, practice showing your work on any multi-step problems, even if you're just studying. Writing out each step you take to solve a problem will help solidify the process in your mind, and you'll be more likely to remember it during the test.

Modality

Modality simply refers to the means or method by which you study. Choosing a study modality that fits your own individual learning style is crucial. No two people learn best in exactly the same way, so it's important to know your strengths and use them to your advantage.

For example, if you learn best by visualization, focus on visualizing a concept in your mind and draw an image or a diagram. Try color-coding your notes, illustrating them, or creating symbols that will trigger your mind to recall a learned concept. If you learn best by hearing or discussing information, find a study partner who learns the same way or read aloud to yourself. Think about how to put the information in your own words. Imagine that you are giving a lecture on the topic and record yourself so you can listen to it later.

For any learning style, flashcards can be helpful. Organize the information so you can take advantage of spare moments to review. Underline key words or phrases. Use different colors for different categories. Mnemonic devices (such as creating a short list in which every item starts with the same letter) can also help with retention. Find what works best for you and use it to store the information in your mind most effectively and easily.

Secret Key #3 – Practice the Right Way

Your success on test day depends not only on how many hours you put into preparing, but also on whether you prepared the right way. It's good to check along the way to see if your studying is paying off. One of the most effective ways to do this is by taking practice tests to evaluate your progress. Practice tests are useful because they show exactly where you need to improve. Every time you take a practice test, pay special attention to these three groups of questions:

- The questions you got wrong
- The questions you had to guess on, even if you guessed right
- The questions you found difficult or slow to work through

This will show you exactly what your weak areas are, and where you need to devote more study time. Ask yourself why each of these questions gave you trouble. Was it because you didn't understand the material? Was it because you didn't remember the vocabulary? Do you need more repetitions on this type of question to build speed and confidence? Dig into those questions and figure out how you can strengthen your weak areas as you go back to review the material.

Additionally, many practice tests have a section explaining the answer choices. It can be tempting to read the explanation and think that you now have a good understanding of the concept. However, an explanation likely only covers part of the question's broader context. Even if the explanation makes perfect sense, **go back and investigate** every concept related to the question until you're positive you have a thorough understanding.

As you go along, keep in mind that the practice test is just that: practice. Memorizing these questions and answers will not be very helpful on the actual test because it is unlikely to have any of the same exact questions. If you only know the right answers to the sample questions, you won't be prepared for the real thing. **Study the concepts** until you understand them fully, and then you'll be able to answer any question that shows up on the test.

It's important to wait on the practice tests until you're ready. If you take a test on your first day of study, you may be overwhelmed by the amount of material covered and how much you need to learn. Work up to it gradually.

On test day, you'll need to be prepared for answering questions, managing your time, and using the test-taking strategies you've learned. It's a lot to balance, like a mental marathon that will have a big impact on your future. Like training for a marathon, you'll need to start slowly and work your way up. When test day arrives, you'll be ready.

Start with the strategies you've read in the first two Secret Keys—plan your course and study in the way that works best for you. If you have time, consider using multiple study resources to get different approaches to the same concepts. It can be helpful to see difficult concepts from more than one angle. Then find a good source for practice tests. Many times, the test website will suggest potential study resources or provide sample tests.

Practice Test Strategy

If you're able to find at least three practice tests, we recommend this strategy:

Untimed and Open-Book Practice

Take the first test with no time constraints and with your notes and study guide handy. Take your time and focus on applying the strategies you've learned.

Timed and Open-Book Practice

Take the second practice test open-book as well, but set a timer and practice pacing yourself to finish in time.

Timed and Closed-Book Practice

Take any other practice tests as if it were test day. Set a timer and put away your study materials. Sit at a table or desk in a quiet room, imagine yourself at the testing center, and answer questions as quickly and accurately as possible.

Keep repeating timed and closed-book tests on a regular basis until you run out of practice tests or it's time for the actual test. Your mind will be ready for the schedule and stress of test day, and you'll be able to focus on recalling the material you've learned.

Secret Key #4 – Pace Yourself

Once you're fully prepared for the material on the test, your biggest challenge on test day will be managing your time. Just knowing that the clock is ticking can make you panic even if you have plenty of time left. Work on pacing yourself so you can build confidence against the time constraints of the exam. Pacing is a difficult skill to master, especially in a high-pressure environment, so **practice is vital**.

Set time expectations for your pace based on how much time is available. For example, if a section has 60 questions and the time limit is 30 minutes, you know you have to average 30 seconds or less per question in order to answer them all. Although 30 seconds is the hard limit, set 25 seconds per question as your goal, so you reserve extra time to spend on harder questions. When you budget extra time for the harder questions, you no longer have any reason to stress when those questions take longer to answer.

Don't let this time expectation distract you from working through the test at a calm, steady pace, but keep it in mind so you don't spend too much time on any one question. Recognize that taking extra time on one question you don't understand may keep you from answering two that you do understand later in the test. If your time limit for a question is up and you're still not sure of the answer, mark it and move on, and come back to it later if the time and the test format allow. If the testing format doesn't allow you to return to earlier questions, just make an educated guess; then put it out of your mind and move on.

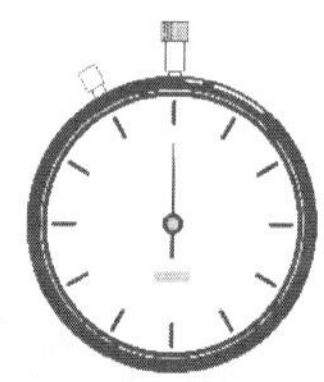

On the easier questions, be careful not to rush. It may seem wise to hurry through them so you have more time for the challenging ones, but it's not worth missing one if you know the concept and just didn't take the time to read the question fully. Work efficiently but make sure you understand the question and have looked at all of the answer choices, since more than one may seem right at first.

Even if you're paying attention to the time, you may find yourself a little behind at some point. You should speed up to get back on track, but do so wisely. Don't panic; just take a few seconds less on each question until you're caught up. Don't guess without thinking, but do look through the answer choices and eliminate any you know are wrong. If you can get down to two choices, it is often worthwhile to guess from those. Once you've chosen an answer, move on and don't dwell on any that you skipped or had to hurry through. If a question was taking too long, chances are it was one of the harder ones, so you weren't as likely to get it right anyway.

On the other hand, if you find yourself getting ahead of schedule, it may be beneficial to slow down a little. The more quickly you work, the more likely you are to make a careless mistake that will affect your score. You've budgeted time for each question, so don't be afraid to spend that time. Practice an efficient but careful pace to get the most out of the time you have.

Secret Key #5 – Have a Plan for Guessing

When you're taking the test, you may find yourself stuck on a question. Some of the answer choices seem better than others, but you don't see the one answer choice that is obviously correct. What do you do?

The scenario described above is very common, yet most test takers have not effectively prepared for it. Developing and practicing a plan for guessing may be one of the single most effective uses of your time as you get ready for the exam.

In developing your plan for guessing, there are three questions to address:

- When should you start the guessing process?
- How should you narrow down the choices?
- Which answer should you choose?

When to Start the Guessing Process

Unless your plan for guessing is to select C every time (which, despite its merits, is not what we recommend), you need to leave yourself enough time to apply your answer elimination strategies. Since you have a limited amount of time for each question, that means that if you're going to give yourself the best shot at guessing correctly, you have to decide quickly whether or not you will guess.

Of course, the best-case scenario is that you don't have to guess at all, so first, see if you can answer the question based on your knowledge of the subject and basic reasoning skills. Focus on the key words in the question and try to jog your memory of related topics. Give yourself a chance to bring the knowledge to mind, but once you realize that you don't have (or you can't access) the knowledge you need to answer the question, it's time to start the guessing process.

It's almost always better to start the guessing process too early than too late. It only takes a few seconds to remember something and answer the question from knowledge. Carefully eliminating wrong answer choices takes longer. Plus, going through the process of eliminating answer choices can actually help jog your memory.

Summary: Start the guessing process as soon as you decide that you can't answer the question based on your knowledge.

How to Narrow Down the Choices

The next chapter in this book (**Test-Taking Strategies**) includes a wide range of strategies for how to approach questions and how to look for answer choices to eliminate. You will definitely want to read those carefully, practice them, and figure out which ones work best for you. Here though, we're going to address a mindset rather than a particular strategy.

Your odds of guessing an answer correctly depend on how many options you are choosing from.

Number of options left	5	4	3	2	1
Odds of guessing correctly	20%	25%	33%	50%	100%

You can see from this chart just how valuable it is to be able to eliminate incorrect answers and make an educated guess, but there are two things that many test takers do that cause them to miss out on the benefits of guessing:

- Accidentally eliminating the correct answer
- Selecting an answer based on an impression

We'll look at the first one here, and the second one in the next section.

To avoid accidentally eliminating the correct answer, we recommend a thought exercise called **the $5 challenge**. In this challenge, you only eliminate an answer choice from contention if you are willing to bet $5 on it being wrong. Why $5? Five dollars is a small but not insignificant amount of money. It's an amount you could afford to lose but wouldn't want to throw away. And while losing $5 once might not hurt too much, doing it twenty times will set you back $100. In the same way, each small decision you make—eliminating a choice here, guessing on a question there—won't by itself impact your score very much, but when you put them all together, they can make a big difference. By holding each answer choice elimination decision to a higher standard, you can reduce the risk of accidentally eliminating the correct answer.

The $5 challenge can also be applied in a positive sense: If you are willing to bet $5 that an answer choice *is* correct, go ahead and mark it as correct.

Summary: Only eliminate an answer choice if you are willing to bet $5 that it is wrong.

Which Answer to Choose

You're taking the test. You've run into a hard question and decided you'll have to guess. You've eliminated all the answer choices you're willing to bet $5 on. Now you have to pick an answer. Why do we even need to talk about this? Why can't you just pick whichever one you feel like when the time comes?

The answer to these questions is that if you don't come into the test with a plan, you'll rely on your impression to select an answer choice, and if you do that, you risk falling into a trap. The test writers know that everyone who takes their test will be guessing on some of the questions, so they intentionally write wrong answer choices to seem plausible. You still have to pick an answer though, and if the wrong answer choices are designed to look right, how can you ever be sure that you're not falling for their trap? The best solution we've found to this dilemma is to take the decision out of your hands entirely. Here is the process we recommend:

Once you've eliminated any choices that you are confident (willing to bet $5) are wrong, select the first remaining choice as your answer.

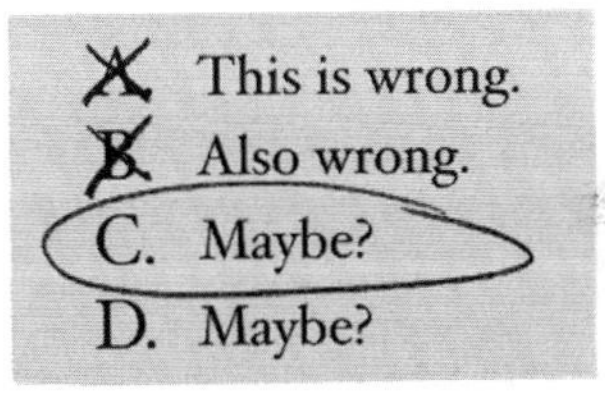

Whether you choose to select the first remaining choice, the second, or the last, the important thing is that you use some preselected standard. Using this approach guarantees that you will not be enticed into selecting an answer choice that looks right, because you are not basing your decision on how the answer choices look.

This is not meant to make you question your knowledge. Instead, it is to help you recognize the difference between your knowledge and your impressions. There's a huge difference between thinking an answer is right because of what you know, and thinking an answer is right because it looks or sounds like it should be right.

Summary: To ensure that your selection is appropriately random, make a predetermined selection from among all answer choices you have not eliminated.

Test-Taking Strategies

This section contains a list of test-taking strategies that you may find helpful as you work through the test. By taking what you know and applying logical thought, you can maximize your chances of answering any question correctly!

It is very important to realize that every question is different and every person is different: no single strategy will work on every question, and no single strategy will work for every person. That's why we've included all of them here, so you can try them out and determine which ones work best for different types of questions and which ones work best for you.

Question Strategies

✓ Read Carefully

Read the question and the answer choices carefully. Don't miss the question because you misread the terms. You have plenty of time to read each question thoroughly and make sure you understand what is being asked. Yet a happy medium must be attained, so don't waste too much time. You must read carefully and efficiently.

✓ Contextual Clues

Look for contextual clues. If the question includes a word you are not familiar with, look at the immediate context for some indication of what the word might mean. Contextual clues can often give you all the information you need to decipher the meaning of an unfamiliar word. Even if you can't determine the meaning, you may be able to narrow down the possibilities enough to make a solid guess at the answer to the question.

✓ Prefixes

If you're having trouble with a word in the question or answer choices, try dissecting it. Take advantage of every clue that the word might include. Prefixes can be a huge help. Usually, they allow you to determine a basic meaning. *Pre-* means before, *post-* means after, *pro-* is positive, *de-* is negative. From prefixes, you can get an idea of the general meaning of the word and try to put it into context.

✓ Hedge Words

Watch out for critical hedge words, such as *likely, may, can, often, almost, mostly, usually, generally, rarely*, and *sometimes*. Question writers insert these hedge phrases to cover every possibility. Often an answer choice will be wrong simply because it leaves no room for exception. Be on guard for answer choices that have definitive words such as *exactly* and *always*.

✓ Switchback Words

Stay alert for *switchbacks*. These are the words and phrases frequently used to alert you to shifts in thought. The most common switchback words are *but, although*, and *however*. Others include *nevertheless, on the other hand, even though, while, in spite of, despite*, and *regardless of*. Switchback words are important to catch because they can change the direction of the question or an answer choice.

⊘ FACE VALUE

When in doubt, use common sense. Accept the situation in the problem at face value. Don't read too much into it. These problems will not require you to make wild assumptions. If you have to go beyond creativity and warp time or space in order to have an answer choice fit the question, then you should move on and consider the other answer choices. These are normal problems rooted in reality. The applicable relationship or explanation may not be readily apparent, but it is there for you to figure out. Use your common sense to interpret anything that isn't clear.

Answer Choice Strategies

⊘ ANSWER SELECTION

The most thorough way to pick an answer choice is to identify and eliminate wrong answers until only one is left, then confirm it is the correct answer. Sometimes an answer choice may immediately seem right, but be careful. The test writers will usually put more than one reasonable answer choice on each question, so take a second to read all of them and make sure that the other choices are not equally obvious. As long as you have time left, it is better to read every answer choice than to pick the first one that looks right without checking the others.

⊘ ANSWER CHOICE FAMILIES

An answer choice family consists of two (in rare cases, three) answer choices that are very similar in construction and cannot all be true at the same time. If you see two answer choices that are direct opposites or parallels, one of them is usually the correct answer. For instance, if one answer choice says that quantity *x* increases and another either says that quantity *x* decreases (opposite) or says that quantity *y* increases (parallel), then those answer choices would fall into the same family. An answer choice that doesn't match the construction of the answer choice family is more likely to be incorrect. Most questions will not have answer choice families, but when they do appear, you should be prepared to recognize them.

⊘ ELIMINATE ANSWERS

Eliminate answer choices as soon as you realize they are wrong, but make sure you consider all possibilities. If you are eliminating answer choices and realize that the last one you are left with is also wrong, don't panic. Start over and consider each choice again. There may be something you missed the first time that you will realize on the second pass.

⊘ AVOID FACT TRAPS

Don't be distracted by an answer choice that is factually true but doesn't answer the question. You are looking for the choice that answers the question. Stay focused on what the question is asking for so you don't accidentally pick an answer that is true but incorrect. Always go back to the question and make sure the answer choice you've selected actually answers the question and is not merely a true statement.

⊘ EXTREME STATEMENTS

In general, you should avoid answers that put forth extreme actions as standard practice or proclaim controversial ideas as established fact. An answer choice that states the "process should be used in certain situations, if..." is much more likely to be correct than one that states the "process should be discontinued completely." The first is a calm rational statement and doesn't even make a definitive, uncompromising stance, using a hedge word *if* to provide wiggle room, whereas the second choice is far more extreme.

☑ Benchmark

As you read through the answer choices and you come across one that seems to answer the question well, mentally select that answer choice. This is not your final answer, but it's the one that will help you evaluate the other answer choices. The one that you selected is your benchmark or standard for judging each of the other answer choices. Every other answer choice must be compared to your benchmark. That choice is correct until proven otherwise by another answer choice beating it. If you find a better answer, then that one becomes your new benchmark. Once you've decided that no other choice answers the question as well as your benchmark, you have your final answer.

☑ Predict the Answer

Before you even start looking at the answer choices, it is often best to try to predict the answer. When you come up with the answer on your own, it is easier to avoid distractions and traps because you will know exactly what to look for. The right answer choice is unlikely to be word-for-word what you came up with, but it should be a close match. Even if you are confident that you have the right answer, you should still take the time to read each option before moving on.

General Strategies

☑ Tough Questions

If you are stumped on a problem or it appears too hard or too difficult, don't waste time. Move on! Remember though, if you can quickly check for obviously incorrect answer choices, your chances of guessing correctly are greatly improved. Before you completely give up, at least try to knock out a couple of possible answers. Eliminate what you can and then guess at the remaining answer choices before moving on.

☑ Check Your Work

Since you will probably not know every term listed and the answer to every question, it is important that you get credit for the ones that you do know. Don't miss any questions through careless mistakes. If at all possible, try to take a second to look back over your answer selection and make sure you've selected the correct answer choice and haven't made a costly careless mistake (such as marking an answer choice that you didn't mean to mark). This quick double check should more than pay for itself in caught mistakes for the time it costs.

☑ Pace Yourself

It's easy to be overwhelmed when you're looking at a page full of questions; your mind is confused and full of random thoughts, and the clock is ticking down faster than you would like. Calm down and maintain the pace that you have set for yourself. Especially as you get down to the last few minutes of the test, don't let the small numbers on the clock make you panic. As long as you are on track by monitoring your pace, you are guaranteed to have time for each question.

☑ Don't Rush

It is very easy to make errors when you are in a hurry. Maintaining a fast pace in answering questions is pointless if it makes you miss questions that you would have gotten right otherwise. Test writers like to include distracting information and wrong answers that seem right. Taking a little extra time to avoid careless mistakes can make all the difference in your test score. Find a pace that allows you to be confident in the answers that you select.

⊘ Keep Moving

Panicking will not help you pass the test, so do your best to stay calm and keep moving. Taking deep breaths and going through the answer elimination steps you practiced can help to break through a stress barrier and keep your pace.

Final Notes

The combination of a solid foundation of content knowledge and the confidence that comes from practicing your plan for applying that knowledge is the key to maximizing your performance on test day. As your foundation of content knowledge is built up and strengthened, you'll find that the strategies included in this chapter become more and more effective in helping you quickly sift through the distractions and traps of the test to isolate the correct answer.

Now that you're preparing to move forward into the test content chapters of this book, be sure to keep your goal in mind. As you read, think about how you will be able to apply this information on the test. If you've already seen sample questions for the test and you have an idea of the question format and style, try to come up with questions of your own that you can answer based on what you're reading. This will give you valuable practice applying your knowledge in the same ways you can expect to on test day.

Good luck and good studying!

Basic Economic Concepts

Capital

Capital is a comprehensive term for all or any methods by which products are made by labor. This includes a wide variety of tools or elements. **Physical capital** may include all categories of real objects such as equipment, plants, land, and machinery that contribute to the process of production. **Intellectual capital** is the necessary ingredient that transforms the production process by human interaction. Included in intellectual capital is the utilization of information, management skills, and technological advances, as well as the application of ideas and theories which are catalysts in the economic system.

Although capital is generally regarded as an essential ingredient of benign economic activity, it can also be used to foster the **defense** of a state or prepare a country for an aggressive war. Large portions of Germany's capital were used by the Nazis in their attempt to dominate Europe. Capital is commonly used to further a state's **geopolitical aims** through peaceful or belligerent goals. The utilization of capital is a prime indicator of any country's goals and ambitions.

Historically, capital was considered to be physical equipment, machinery, plants, and other major investments used in manufacturing. The more modern concept of capital broadens the definition to include a wide range of **assets** that are utilized in the production process.

Financial capitalrepresents the operating funds and monetary investment in a business or plant. Financial capital is often obtained by corporations through the issue of stock in exchange for funds. Natural resources such as oceans, forests, mountains, and rivers provide **natural capital** which may or may not be publicly owned. Capital that is used to provide support systems for fundamental production processes and operating ability is sometimes termed **infrastructural capital**. Much of this type of capital is represented in plants and equipment. The abilities and acumen gained from education and experience are sometimes referred to as **human capital**. This incorporates the many types of growth and development from what we call human resources.

Factors of Production

Resources that are used in the production and manufacture of goods and services are called **factors of production**. They include land and natural products derived from land, including dirt, gems, minerals, and fodder. The cost of using land is usually rent in one form or another. Labor is another factor of production, and this is a blanket term for all individuals involved in the manufacturing, marketing, and transfer of goods and services. The payment for labor is designated as wages. Capital is the third essential factor of production. These definitions of the factors of production are from classical economics and political economy, and they remain accurate today, although the idea of capital has been expanded to include human expertise and technology.

Foundation of Economics as a Science

The study of economics includes **microeconomics**, which is concerned with smaller units, such as individuals and firms, and **macroeconomics**, which looks at the economy as a composite, taking a more global view. In general, economics deals with topics such as scarcity, supply, demand, and choices made by various parts of the economy and the total economy. There are a variety of economic topics that overlap both microeconomics and macroeconomics. These hybrid areas may be covered separately or as a part of the micro/macroeconomic spectrum. "Mainstream" economics is a blend of macroeconomics and economic theory developed in the last 50 years. This includes a number of schools of economic thought, each with its own assumptions, conclusions, and methodology. Economics centers on the idea of scarce resources and how to best utilize these resources to meet the needs of individuals and the economic system as a whole.

Mechanism Where the Study of Economics Occurs

The exchange of services and goods in an organized marketplace, where sellers and buyers vie to optimize their results by trading, is the **mechanism where the study of economics occurs**. Factors of production, the directed use of labor and capital, and the achievement of profit are the driving forces of an economic system. The clearest representation of these elements occurs in a **free market economy**, of which capitalism is the prime example. These factors are also in play in **state-controlled systems**, which include communism and socialism. Many contend that in all economic systems, the driving force is self-interest, or the "Invisible Hand" that Adam Smith defined in his Wealth of Nations. Economics may be studied in a wide spectrum of political, social, and financial systems. Commonalities and contrasts may be used as a method of comparing economic theory in a variety of settings. Many of the crucial components of economics are active in any organized society, regardless of its philosophy.

Beginnings of Economics as a Science

Political economy was defined as the economics of **competing states**, and was the term used by early economic thinkers. Neoclassical economists discarded this term in the late 1800s in favor of simply *economics*. The origin of the term *economics* is from the Greek word *oikonomikos*, meaning settlement laws. Economics was a recognized field in early Greek, Arab, and Roman eras. This is known as the **premodern period**. The mercantile and physiocrat systems are termed **early modern**, and what we now call economics is named **modern economics** in the history of economic thought. The pioneers of modern economic thought include such giants as Karl Marx, David Ricardo, John Stuart Mill, and of course, Adam Smith. Economic references and problems are discussed in early texts such as the Old and New Testaments. Economic thought has often played an important part in political systems such as Communism and Socialism and has played a major role in all societies.

Foundation of Modern Economics

Modern economics is based on one basic premise: that **resources** are scarce and limited, and that **choices** must be made in the acquisition and use of them. All other questions and alternatives flow from this assumption. Economic choices involve sacrificing something in order to obtain another thing. This sacrifice is called the "**opportunity cost**" of the choice. You may choose to spend your last dollar on a candy bar rather than a writing tablet, thus the opportunity cost of the candy bar is the tablet. There are seemingly endless choices in a consumer society, all of which involve choices and opportunity costs. The choices and opportunity costs are expressed in price relationships in modern economics. Each individual makes many economic decisions (choices) each day, and the aggregate reflects the economic activity of a society. Choices are driven by the **utility**, or want-satisfying abilities of the goods and services. Choices are ranked on the ability of the good or service to fill a perceived need of the individual. This utility function is active in most, but not all, economic choices.

Scarcity and Choice

Economics could rightfully be called the study of **scarcity**. Limited resources are available to satisfy the wants and needs of both individuals and states. Economics involves the **choices** made by an economy to satisfy these wants and needs. Every economy must choose what goods and services to produce, how to produce them, and for whom they are intended. Limitations of the factors of production—land, labor, and capital—sometimes make these choices difficult. When an economic choice is made, there is an "**opportunity cost**" implicit in the choice. The opportunity cost is what is given up by making a choice. If a country chooses to manufacture automobiles, it may not have the industrial capacity to produce tanks or aircraft. Thus, the economic choice to make automobiles involves the opportunity cost of not making tanks or aircraft. Individuals and countries continually make economic choices and sacrifice opportunist costs in the process. An individual may choose to attend a film rather than go out to dinner. Choices are driven by what people and countries feel is in their best interest.

Specialization and Division of Labor

Labor, a major factor of production, must be used in the most efficient manner to optimize the economic system. The concept of **specialization** requires that labor (and other factors of production) be used on work on which they are most efficient in order to produce goods in the most cost-effective manner. This means allocating specialized operations to various members of the workforce so each can concentrate on what he or she does best. The result should be an increase in productivity with a corresponding increased profitability of the firm. When this concept is extrapolated throughout an economy, it provides a country with a competitive advantage, that is to say, a nation, company, or individual will be producing most efficiently, giving a boost to productivity. Such an economy will tend to have an edge in international trade, and function more efficiently in the domestic economy.

Market Economy

A market economy is an economic system in which the **individuals** own and operate all factors related to production. It relies on **entrepreneurship** to spur markets for operation. The goal of individuals in a market economy is to obtain a profit from their chosen area of business. It is often associated with capitalism and private ownership of capital. Market economies are successful in part due to increased individual freedom for their members. When people have the freedom to make their own decisions, the economy is more likely to function efficiently. This is because changes in the markets will be noticed and responded to quickly and appropriately. There is more flexibility for economic action in a market economy system. Through private ownership and individual freedom, market economies are the most successful systems for the operations of free markets in the world. The largest market economies today are the United States, China, and Japan.

Review Video: Basics of Market Economy
Visit mometrix.com/academy and enter code: 791556

Economics in the Premodern Age

Ibn Khaldun of Tunis, writing in the 12th century, discussed political and economic theory. A favorite subject of his was population density and its effect on economic cycles. This is one of the earliest records of economic theory. **Scholasticism**, a theological school of philosophy in the Middle Ages, incorporated a debate over a number of basic economic issues, including how a fair price of something could be determined. In the wars between the Church and her reformers during the **Reformation**, the concept of free trade arose and was considered in both theological and political contexts. The church and nobility saw economic activity as a way to raise revenues, and imposed taxes on almost all transactions. These taxes were used to finance wars and enrich the ruling classes, almost never benefiting those being taxed. **Feudalism** imposed its own system of economics, determining how most economic affairs would be conducted and taxed. Needless to say, the serfs rarely saw any good from these measures.

Early Stirrings of Economic Thought

The **Mercantilists**, a group of European importers and exporters, strove to profit from exploring new markets, trading goods at a profitable rate, and growing their markets. Mercantilists were the dominant economic force in the new nation-states of Europe. Their activities were instrumental in leading to the discovery and settlement of the New World. The **Physiocrats**, a school of eco-philosophy active in France during the Enlightenment, were led by writers such as Anne Turgot and Francois Quesnay. Arguably, this was the first school or movement that viewed economics as a field in its own right. Many believe that modern economics was founded by the Physiocrats. Later thinkers and writers such as Adam Smith and David Ricardo built their theories on the foundation laid by the Physiocrats. As a group, the Physiocrats were short-lived, but their impact was significant in the development of economic thought.

Timeline of Economic Schools of Thought Through the Centuries

Schools of economic thought may be loosely categorized as follows:

- **16th-18th Century** - Dominated by the European nation-states who pioneered Mercantilism in an effort to enrich themselves through trade and exploration of new markets. The Physiocrats were an important 18th-century economic school that originated in France.
- **18th-19th Century** - Great economic thinkers and philosophers such as Adam Smith, John Stuart Mill, Thomas Malthus, and David Ricardo wrote important works that provided the foundation for Classical economics. This period also saw the rise of the "Utopian Socialists," who formulated economic ideas to cure the ills of society. Marxism is also included in this period, although it mixes political, social, and economic theory in a hybrid philosophy.
- **Late 19th Century** - Alfred Marshall is felt to be the father of Neoclassical economics. Marshall authored the concept of "marginal theory of value," which is the cornerstone of neoclassical economics.
- **20th Century** - Carl Menger wrote the seminal work on economics for what was to be called the Austrian school. The American Institutionalist school and German school of economics appeared during this period.

Principle of Comparative Advantage

Why would two countries continue to trade if one can produce goods and services cheaper than another? The answer is a **comparative advantage**, which depends upon the ratio between the costs of producing different products. This concept was introduced by **David Ricardo** in his seminal work on political economy and trade. Essentially, the principle states that each nation should specialize in producing the commodity with the lower opportunity cost. This would give the country a comparative advantage in exporting that product. It should trade with another country for a product for which it has a comparative disadvantage. Thus, each country will benefit from buying goods abroad that are more costly to produce at home. **Competitive advantage** is the principle that makes international commerce work effectively. If a country does not have a competitive advantage in a product, there must be other reasons for that country to trade.

Command Economy

A command economy is one in which the government controls basic economic activities. Such an economy is directed by decisions of one group (the ruling class) for all members of the society. Such a system, typical in dictatorships, suffers because of the lack of private interest in economic success. Command economies are slower to respond to changing economic fluctuations, as they are controlled by cumbersome organizations and not responsive to the "invisible hand" of self-interest. Socialism and communism are examples of command economies today.

Marginalism

Marginalism concerns itself with the economic worth of the last (or next) product or service provided. The cost of making the last product, the cost of hiring the last employee, and the cost of selling the last product, determine the **marginal cost** of that next good. Presumably, a company will continue to produce goods and services until it becomes unprofitable. Production will cease when the marginal return of a product does not yield a profit. From the consumer's viewpoint, the **marginal utility** of the purchase is the crucial factor. How much satisfaction does an individual get from each purchase? When this marginal utility decreases too much, the buyer will not buy the next unit. The idea of diminishing returns often determines how many units of a good or service a buyer will purchase. For example, after eating a piece of pie, the want-satisfying power of the next piece of pie is decreased. When this marginal utility reaches a certain point, the consumer will stop buying.

Opportunity Cost

The opportunity cost of an economic decision is the loss of potential gain from other opportunities when one opportunity is taken. For example, a person may have enough money for a vacation in Europe or a new car but not both. The **opportunity cost** of buying the car will be the trip to Europe. These decisions are made usually on the **utility** of each choice. In other words, determining which choice would provide the most pleasure to the consumer. In a complex economy, there are many competing factors that provide utility. An individual, firm, or government will always choose what they perceive to be the best choice given limited resources. These choices are usually not clear-cut, and many factors go into some economic decisions. This is more common when companies or governments have to choose between a number of needed and attractive choices. Different parts of society will have different ideas about the best way to use their resources.

Criticisms of Marginality

Marginal utility is founded on **subjectivity**, rather than **objectivity**. Marginal utility places its focus on buying and selling transactions between individual units in the economy, to the exclusion of the activity of the economy as a whole. The marketplace is the Holy Grail for the proponents of marginal utility, who see the markets as the foundation of economic activity. The production function is ignored; this is a crucial error, as costs of production are a major determinant of prices, and, therefore, all microeconomic activity. Critics of marginal utility say it is impossible to understand **consumer utility**, which is determined in part by prices. The prices themselves are based on consumer preferences, making an accurate analysis difficult if not impossible. Another area of criticism for the concept of marginal utility is that it often attempts to correlate utility with price. This correlation does not hold true where a product may be useful and necessary to an individual but cost nothing. An example of this would be water.

Production in Depth

The production function in microeconomics refers to the total process of **producing or assembling** goods and services that are to be traded in a marketplace. Production decisions are some of the most vital in microeconomics. A firm or individual must decide what to make and how many units to provide. This will often depend on the method of production and the unit price of making each product. An evaluation of the necessary resources to be utilized is another important production decision. In tandem with sophisticated market research, optimum decisions can be made about producing goods and services. Production is a process, and, as such, it occurs through time and space. Because it is a flow concept, an important statistic is the amount of production for a specific period of time. Other factors of concern are the amount and physical dimensions of the finished process. This will be important in storing and shipping the finished goods.

Efficiency and X-Efficiency

The measurement of the productivity of a production process is vital. Productivity may be said to be **efficient** when the optimum number of finished products is produced with a minimum of raw materials, assuming quality control is maintained. If a production operation is less productive than anticipated, due to internal or external forces, it is said to be **X-efficient**. Such X-efficient production operations are often due to a number of factors beyond the control of the producer. Examples would be shortages of raw materials, increased and unexpected competition, or problems in the supply of necessary labor. The productivity of a production function is simply based on how many units of a finished product can be made from a minimum amount of inputs. The more efficient processes give firms an important competitive position and greater flexibility in pricing and marketing. Decisions made about production will often determine the success or failure of the product line for a firm.

Factors of Production

Factors of production are the sum total of the resources needed to produce finished goods. The major **factors** identified by economists include the use of land (for factories and agricultural products), labor (the human workforce), natural resources (raw materials used in manufacturing), and capital goods (previously manufactured equipment used in production). Human inputs such as management and human relations could be added to the mix. Contemporary economists often include technological expertise in the factors of production. Factors of production may be **fixed** (one which cannot be changed) or **variable** (one which can be adjusted by management easily). Examples of fixed factors would be physical plants, heavy machinery, and key managerial personnel. A variable factor of production is one whose usage rate can be changed easily. In the "long run" all of these factors of production can be adjusted by management. The "short run," however, is defined as a period in which at least one of the factors of production is fixed.

Diminishing Marginal Returns Analysis

As additional raw materials and resources are added to production factors, a point occurs where the production function becomes less efficient. In other words, additional resources are yielding less-profitable final products. This point is called the **point of diminishing returns** and is measured as a position on the marginal physical production curve. Continuing production will eventually result in producing products that lose money. Thus, it would be preferable to stop production. **Diminishing marginal returns** will vary from industry to industry, depending on the necessary factors of production needed to produce goods and services. The combination of land, labor, and capital needed for production is different for each product, so the point of diminishing marginal return will also differ. Demand, supply, and price changes in the factors of production will all impact this analysis.

Production Functions

Production functions, an important area of analysis in microeconomics, concerns itself with the ratio of raw materials or resources needed to produce a certain amount of goods and services. This relationship may be depicted as a mathematical one or illustrated with a graph. The goal of analyzing the production functions is to **optimize** the number of finished goods that can be obtained from the minimum of inputs. Many factors enter into such an analysis, including supply and demand of the factors of production, state-of-the-art technology, and managerial skill. Every production function will be different because of the mix of factors for producing different goods at various times. If a producer knows the exact quantity of finished goods he or she must manufacture, the **production function** would be the **minimum necessary resources** needed to achieve that production number. Current technology will affect this combination of resources. In this type of analysis, costs and prices are not considered.

Criticism

Controversy has surrounded the validity of production function analysis. Most of the **criticism** is concerned with how certain factors of production were measured and how proportions of the factors were mixed. Some economists feel it is not possible to post a necessary amount of capital without a complete understanding of both interest rates and the cost of labor. The production function analysis must include specific prices for all factors of production, but the analysis itself depends on knowing these variables. This is the "which came first, the chicken or the egg" problem. Exact variables cannot be known until the production function analysis is complete, but the analysis is the method of determining the variables. Special mathematical constructs and assumptions must be built in these models of production functioned to have a useful function.

Production Possibility Curve

When any product is made, there is an opportunity cost of forgoing using the resources to make a different product. If two or more items are being produced at the same time, there will be **opportunity costs** involved in decisions regarding the relative amount of each product to produce. This analysis is called the **production possibility curve**. The production possibility curve is a valuable tool for manufacturers because it explores production alternatives and their economic result. Points of **maximum productivity** may be plotted using this graphical tool, which will also illuminate when production becomes **inefficient**. Companies can then choose optimum mixes of products as well as determine when a finished good is not economically feasible to manufacture. The analysis should yield the necessary information for a firm to adjust their product mix and quantities of goods produced to the most profitable level.

Cost-Benefit Analysis

The determination of the best possible economic action in a situation is often formally or intuitively a result of a **cost-benefit computation**. An individual must ask what the total costs will be in any decision in relation to the total benefits, which may be reasonably predicted. Analyzing several alternatives using this approach will yield the best decision given the information available. In business decisions, this usually means determining what amount of resources must be used to gain a specified return or profit. Such cost-benefit calculations are not limited to money. Subjective factors must be considered and sometimes an arbitrary monetary value placed on them. Economic decisions, particularly on the part of governments, must weigh economic, quality-of-life, political, and social elements into this analysis. For example, a government decision to drill for oil in a natural habitat will include economic considerations, as well as the impact of the decision on the well-being of the society as a whole. Since almost all economic actions occur over time, future costs and profits must be considered from a **present-value perspective**.

Consumer Preference

Microeconomics is concerned with individual decisions that ultimately affect the entire economy. Consumer behavior is an important aspect of microeconomics. **Consumer preferences** are difficult to assess, because of the seemingly endless choices, conscious and unconscious, that motivate consumer behavior. Economic models have been constructed to better understand consumer activities. These are sometimes called **preference relations** (charting consumers' preferences). These models of consumer preferences have many flaws, but they can attempt to predict the behavior of buyers under various sets of conditions. A major flaw may be termed the completeness of understanding consumer behavior. Although a preference model may be able to show in theory how consumers will behave under a set of economic conditions, it is impossible to measure all the factors that enter into choices made by buyers. These choices are subject to rapid change due to external economic changes.

Determining Ideal Firm Size

Determining the optimum size of a company provides a challenge for managers. Because businesses are measured, in large part, by their profitability, the size of a firm should ideally be that which provides the **greatest profit**. This size will vary greatly between various companies, industries, and geographical locations. The ideal size of a firm is a fluid variable, changing with economic and competitive fluctuations. Economies and diseconomies of scale, scope, and agglomeration will all contribute to the determination of an **ideal business size**. Particular industries tend to affect the size of firms. For example, manufacturers of heavy equipment, with large labor and capital demands, tend to be larger than candy manufacturers, whose needs differ dramatically. Managers must constantly be attentive to their business' competitive position, costs, market share, and growth potential to adequately predict the ideal size of their companies. A fluid business environment makes these decisions difficult but crucial.

History of Money

Money has been defined as any store of value which has **intrinsic value** or is a **representation** of a store of value (banknotes). Money is the lifeblood of **market transactions**, serving as a measure of value, a medium of exchange, and a convention of accounting. As a means to exchange value for goods and services, money has no peer. But for this to be the case, money must have a guaranteed and obvious value of its own. Historically, commodities including crops and livestock were the first forms of money. When money became accepted as a representation of commodities, the market system was revolutionized. It made trading easy, and quickly became an accepted medium of exchange. In earlier times, money represented the commodities of precious metals, notably gold and silver. In modern economies, money depends on the guarantee of the government to honor its value. These guarantees permit international trade without risk about the value of the money involved.

Forms of Money

The first items considered as "money" were commodities that were traded under a **barter system**. The next advance in the form of money was the minting of **coins** of precious metals, usually silver and gold. This form of money had intrinsic value but was a very limited resource. It could be transported fairly easily in moderate amounts and was difficult to forge. The next leap in the form of money was the advent of **paper notes**, issued and guaranteed by governments. In modern economies, money has taken on a variety of new forms, some a result of increasing technological advances. Modern economies feature paper notes backed by the central bank and government that issues them. Coins with a small percentage of silver or gold are also assets honored by central banks. The intrinsic value of precious metals in most coins is negligible. By far the most revolutionary change in the form of money has occurred in the last 100 years. Demand deposits, credit cards, commercial paper, certificates of deposit, mortgages, and public and private promissory notes are all a form of money today.

John Maynard Keynes

Perhaps the most influential economist of the last 100 years was **John Maynard Keynes**. Born in 1883, Keynes lived his life and developed his theories in England during the first quarter of the 20th century. Although a great proponent of government intervention in managing the economy, Keynes was strongly opposed to socialism, which he felt would weaken a free economy. Keynes's major concerns were the management and control of business cycles, eliminating both depressions and inflation, which he saw as destabilizing economic systems. His major thesis was that **aggregate**

demand was the most important indicator of economic cycles, particularly the extremes of depression and runaway inflation.

Keynes summarized his theories in *The General Theory of Employment, Interest, and Money*, which he wrote in the early 1930s. Keynes's ideas gained international acclaim and were the basis for the active government role in combating the depression in the 1930s. His ideas appeal to those who believe the responsibility of the government is to act strongly to encourage economic growth.

Robert Lucas Jr.

Robert Lucas Jr. is regarded as one of the most important contemporary economists. A professor of Economics at the University of Chicago, Lucas was instrumental in applying microeconomic analytical methods to study the economy as a whole. His work on the theory of "**Rational Expectations**" was groundbreaking and added greatly to his reputation as a leading economist. He was awarded the Nobel Prize for this work in 1995. The "**Lucas Technique**" investigates the dynamic relationships in an economy. It analyzes the cause-and-effect determination of such economic indicators as employment, inflation, government policies in economics, and the role of monetary policy in affecting economic activity. Creator of the famous "**Lucas islands**" model of monetary influence among consumers, he has earned a place of international respect from economists all over the world. Lucas remains an active researcher and economic theorist today.

Robert Mundell

Robert Mundell is another leading contemporary macroeconomist. A professor at Columbia University, Mundell is a leading figure in the development of **supply-side economics**. He was awarded the Nobel Prize in Economics in 1999 for his overall contributions to economic theory. Mundell pioneered theory on **optimal currency areas**, which reflected his interest in the role of currencies in the economic fluctuations of countries. This work established him as an expert on money and currency, and Mundell was active in the development of the **euro** for the European Union. His work in advocating supply-side economics is well known, and he is known as a leading expert on the gold standard and its historical implications. Mundell was hailed as a prophet when he accurately predicted the rampant inflation of the 1970s. He has developed several important economic models, including the **Mundell-Fleming model** and the **Mundell-Tobin effect**.

Finn Erling Kydland

A Norwegian economist who won the Nobel Prize in Economics in 2004 for his research and models of macroeconomic systems, **Kydland** currently holds a teaching position at the University of California. Kydland has immersed himself in the study of the impact of government economic policy over a period of years. His work on the understanding of the **fluctuations of business cycles** is classic, and he is regarded as a pioneer in applying **mathematical models** to the analysis of economic activity. A leading thinker in political economy and macroeconomics, Kydland has done primary and secondary research on the effects of fiscal and monetary policy on business cycles. Labor economics is another specialty of his, and he is regarded as one of the most important of the labor economists. The relationships between the availability, cost, and demand for labor on economic cycles are of paramount interest to Kydland.

Edward Prescott

A major macroeconomist of the day is **Edward Prescott**. A close collaborator of Finn Kydland, with whom he shared the Nobel Prize in economics in 2004, Prescott currently serves as an economist for the Federal Reserve System. He has concentrated his economic interests in the areas of **general equilibrium** and **fluctuations of economic activity**. His particular field of interest is the role of central banks in applying monetary policy to affect business cycles. He addresses the question of whether central banks should be given wide-ranging power to increase or decrease the money supply in an attempt to avoid economic extremes. Prescott developed the **Hodrick-Prescott model of strategies** to even the ups and downs of business cycles. This was widely hailed by economists as a major breakthrough in the management of economic fluctuations in an economy. Prescott currently engages in monetary and fiscal research, as well as holding several teaching positions in economics.

Developmental Economics

Developing countries have unique economic problems that more sophisticated economies do not. Particularly important is the area of long-term economic growth in developing economies. This field is called **developmental economics**. It also includes the microeconomic analyses of individuals and firms in such fledgling economies. It is a highly analytical field that uses **econometrics** (mathematical applications to economics) to predict economic patterns. Usually, both mathematical and qualitative tools are used to measure and predict economic activity in developing countries. Included in the field are the problems of long-term debt and the action of international economic agencies such as the International Monetary Fund. The problem of encouraging and sustaining economic growth in such countries is a primary objective of economists. The field includes not only economic issues and tools but also social and political methods to influence the whole society.

Political Economy

Political economics is an umbrella term that includes a wide variety of economic approaches to study and predict behavior. It often uses techniques and tools from other social sciences in its applications. **Political economy** is a maverick in economic theory, as it often contravenes accepted economic doctrine. Interdisciplinary by definition, political economy studies the interactions of social and political factors on economic issues that affect markets. The term was originally used in political science to compare and contrast relationships of geopolitics between countries. A number of political-social-economic schools have made political economy their main interest. The historical long-term implications of political economy are of great interest to economic historians.

Transport, Exchange, Infrastructure, and Consumption

Transportation is the network that allows the economy to function. Capital and labor must be moved to land in order to facilitate production. Finished goods must be moved through channels of distribution to be available to consumers. **Transport** is necessary for the movement of products, people, and capital. **Economic exchange** is the basic activity of economics. The circular cycle of exchange from consumer to suppliers and back are the transactions that move an economy. The field of exchange is the marketplace, and money is the medium through which these transactions move. Building an **infrastructure** for market transactions is necessary to allow an orderly and dependable mechanism for economic exchange. **Consumption** of goods, services, and ancillary products is the final activity for satisfying the needs and wants of society. Consumption also may include the less tangible qualities of health, leisure activity, goodwill, and freedom of choice.

Disposal

All excess products of consumption or production must be eliminated as **waste**. The failure to dispose of these waste products will result in an impaired economy and a degradation of the quality of life. Waste removal requires a large physical capacity and the employment of significant capital resources. The increasing urbanization of the world makes **waste disposal** an important priority. Systems of waste removal include garbage and sewage operations as well as preventative measures of recycling and legislation to protect the environment. Governments must take responsibility for waste removal because of the scope of the problem. The ecological movement and "green" economics of the past 30 years have raised questions on the economics of waste and the quality of life. This has generated increased concern about such issues as destruction of natural habitats, global warming, air and water pollution, and the importance of sustaining our natural resources.

"The Market"

The central arena of political economy is the **marketplace** where economic activity occurs. It is also the intersecting point of the sometimes competing economic interests and forces at play. Common causes may be found by unlikely allies, and groups may be pitted against each other for economic advantage. In a **capitalistic economic system**, the major task of the state is the creation and preservation of capital and the economic choices involved in its allocation. **Socialism** maintains that decisions and implementation of production should be determined by the power of the state, ostensibly to create the greatest good for the most people. This philosophy brings socialism into conflict with capitalism, which requires that fundamental economic power should be in private hands. **Communism** seeks control over all factors of production as well as political and social dominance over its society.

"Adaptive Expectations"

When individuals base their expectations on past economic events and history, it is called "**adaptive expectations**." An example would be if the stock market has been strong for a period of time, the public will have positive expectations for future advances. Individuals will base their future economic decisions on the cumulative experience of recent economic activity. These decisions will become self-fulfilling if consumers are pessimistic about the future of the economy. An example of adaptive expectations is the general attitude regarding inflation. In the United States, as well as most of the free world, inflation has become a fact of economic life. The expectation of rising prices, increasing wages, and general cost-of-living increases has bred a culture of inflationary expectation that rarely fails to materialize. Sometimes, general pessimism about the economy serves as a deterrent to economic expansion. This is another example of adaptive expectations at work.

Gresham's Law

When two or more types of money are commonly used in an economy, and each is assigned the same value by the country, problems may arise. **Thomas Gresham**, a 15th-century English financial genius, stated that money that has a market value lower than its buying power will drive out a form of money that has **stronger consumption value**. People will tend to keep this "good money" as a store of value and spend the "bad money" to exchange for goods and services. This situation can only happen if two different forms of money are in circulation and the state decrees them to have equal value, when in fact they do not. Given a choice of exchanging good or bad money for goods and services people will always spend the bad money and retain the good money. Thus, as **Gresham's law** states, bad money will drive good money out of circulation. This becomes a serious economic problem if people are hoarding good money as a store of value and using bad money in the marketplace. Soon, all the good money will disappear as people hoard it.

Consumption

When a resource is used and eliminated, it has been **consumed**. Consumption is an important feature of economics, usually meaning personal consumption of goods and services. Consumption has its own determinants, including economic expectations, level of disposable income, and the propensity to consume. Ultimately consumption is a component of aggregate demand in economic theory. Economics makes a clear distinction between **production**, the supplying of goods and services, and the **consumption** of these goods and services. Economic research into consumption raises questions regarding the motivation and reasons for various levels of consumption. The relatively recent importance of our consumer society has placed this element of economic theory under the microscope of analysis. Consumption in all its forms has developed a significant impact on the lives of everyone in a modern economy.

Labor Economics

As in all the factors of production, **labor** has a separate market based on supply and demand. The interaction between employers and workers is the frame of reference of **labor economics**. The result of these interactions affect labor economics and determine income, employment, and wage levels. Labor economics is a vital field since most countries include maximized employment as an economic priority. When labor economics is studied through the individuals and their role in labor markets, microeconomic methods are used. The larger interactions between labor markets and the demand for goods and services, production, consumption, and investment fall under macroeconomic analysis. Both are necessary and useful methods for evaluating the role that labor plays in economic activity. Most of us are more aware of the macroeconomics of labor, which tends to be in the news more often as trends of unemployment and productivity.

Commodity Markets

Commodities are raw or unfinished components of finished goods yet to be produced. Agricultural products such as soybeans, cotton, and wheat are commodities. Separate markets exist for almost all commodities. Currencies of various countries are also traded as commodities in their own markets. Futures markets exist on many heavily traded commodities, where speculation fuels trading for future delivery of products paid for now. Commodities were one of the first classes of goods traded between countries. Modern **commodity markets** have been safeguarded by a bevy of rules and regulations ensuring prompt and accurate payment between countries. International agencies, such as the Bank for International Settlements, regulate transaction settlements, insure currencies, set reserve requirements, and generally reduce risks in trade inherent between countries.

Store of Value

Any form of money or capital including commodities may be seen as a **store of value** if it meets certain standards. Any store of value must be readily stored, retrieved, and saved. The store of value must retain its value over time, both as intrinsic wealth and the ability to use it to settle debts. Many assets have been used as a store of value over the centuries. Precious metals, primarily gold and silver, have been historical favorites. The most stable currencies extant at a historical point also may serve as a store of value. When the British Empire was powerful, the pound sterling was often used as the store of value. Real estate has always been known as a reliable store of value, and art, antiques, and rare collections have also served this purpose. Many of these are not practical for daily trading, which includes immediate settling of accounts. The common feature is that they all have **intrinsic value** and rarely lose it. There is always a more or less stable demand for these items.

High Technology Economics

Many economists and investors feel that the sector of the economy using cutting-edge **high technological methods** is the most promising for economic growth. This conclusion has promoted increasing and sometimes speculative investment in high-tech fields. But as the world learned from the anticipated boom in information technology, reality does not always meet expectations. The so-called "dot-com" boom in the last 20 years saw the making of great fortunes but also the loss of investments when companies failed to meet their expected growth. High technology economics still offers uncommon rewards for the astute investor, but must also be regarded as very high risk for investors. Areas usually associated with high technology advances include nanotechnology, information technology, and biotechnology, among many others. High technology industries flourish across the world, making constant progress in developing new techniques and applications for multiple growth industries.

The Invisible Hand

One of the fundamental concepts of classical economics is the "**invisible guiding hand of self-interest**" that posits each individual will make economic decisions based on his or her best interests. Developed by **Adam Smith**, the father of capitalism and leading classical economist, the theory states that individuals acting in their own self-interest will also promote the general welfare of all members of the society. Smith felt this was a social mechanism that tended to benefit all. Smith's argument was based on his belief that in a free market economy, people tend to produce goods in demand by consumers. He did not necessarily feel that all self-interested action by itself benefited all of society. Smith's original observations and conclusions are a foundation of classical economics and have been incorporated in one form or another in many schools of economics. Much of **macroeconomic theory** uses the invisible hand concept in postulating economic behavior.

Cost-Of-Production Theory of Value

The concept that the value of an object represents the sum total of all the resources that were involved in producing it is called the **cost-of-production theory of value**. This cost would include any and all of the factors of production utilized in producing the good. Classical economists support the **labor theory-of-value** ideas of Adam Smith, David Ricardo, and Karl Marx. Marx's theory is flawed by his inclusion of the surplus component of value unrelated to the production process. Most contemporary economists reject the cost-of-production theory of value in favor of the marginal theory of value, which contends that an economic value is determined by the marginal utility derived by the consumer in using the product. Some economists distinguish between sectors with **cost-determined** prices and values and **demand-determined** value, which is set by the level of aggregate demand.

Laissez-Faire

The term *laissez-faire* is derived from the French imperative *lassier faire*, meaning to "let do," indicating a hands-off approach. Historically, the term was used by the physiocrats who demanded less governmental influence on international trade. It has become a catch-all phrase for allowing the market the freedom inherent in transactions, without outside influences. Classical economics found a supporter for ***laissez-faire*** in Adam Smith, although he had reservations about some aspects of the policy. A broader definition of *laissez-faire* reflects a style of leadership that allows maximum freedom of individuals to act on their own initiative rather than following orders routinely. It empowers subordinates to make independent decisions and take action on their own. Critics of *laissez-faire* economics point out the failures of lack of any control on economic affairs. The 1920s are sometimes cited as a period in which a lack of government safeguards plunged the country into the Great Depression.

Information Economics

The sub-branch of economics which deals with the use of information in making economic policy and decisions is called **information economics**. Information has unique qualities, being wildly inaccurate at times, easily accessible, and difficult to fully believe. A prime element in economic decisions, information makes accurate and valid choices difficult at times. Information economics studies the mechanisms of economic technology, the value of economic information and its applications, and the asymmetries of information in economics. The market for information is unique. Information is presumably for sale to anyone who will buy it, and it can be sold multiple times. Information has virtually no marginal cost to the buyer. It is easy to duplicate and may be resold many times over. Sometimes information is sold as a bundle. Various sources and pieces of information are combined and sold with or without commentary or suggestions.

Reaganomics

The term *Reaganomics* is an umbrella description of the economic policy of the Reagan administration from 1980-1988. These policies faced very high inflation rates and increasing unemployment, a combination called **stagflation**. These dual problems were addressed by applying the principles of **supply-side economics**, combining tax reductions with decreased government spending. Liberal economists and politicians bemoaned the approach as helping the wealthy at the expense of middle- and lower-income individuals. Supply-side economics attempts to encourage investment and expansion through tax cuts and austerity programs rather than stimulating demand. This is the idea of the "trickle-down" approach of economic well-being, beginning at the top. The twin problems of inflation and unemployment were largely solved during the Reagan years, but there is hot debate whether this was caused by economic policy or simply a turn in the business cycle.

Thomas Malthus and "Dismal Science"

Thomas Malthus, the 18th-century economist who named economics the "**dismal science**," felt that population would grow at a rate that would cause people to starve, and the level of population would reach a subsistence level. Malthus's theories have been proved wrong in a large part of the developed world, but his predictions are accurate for many poor third-world countries who suffer periodic **famines**. Industrialized countries have developed technologies to produce food to keep abreast of population growth, which has been slowed by birth control methods. Developing countries with unchecked population explosions and inferior technology often cannot produce enough food to feed themselves. These countries must rely on international aid and relief agencies to provide the essentials of life. Much of the development of third-world nations is geared to increasing food production and introducing methods to slow the population growth. These actions have had mixed success to date.

Significant Literature in Economics

The Wealth of Nations - Adam Smith

The book is usually considered to be the beginning of **modern economics**. It begins with a discussion of the Industrial Revolution. Later, it critiques mercantilism and a synthesis of the emerging economic thinking of his time. It is mostly known due to the idea of **The Invisible Hand**, which means that people will unintentionally improve their community through the pursuit of their own wants and needs.

Das Kapital - Karl Marx

Das Kapital is a political-economic treatise by Karl Marx. The book is a critical analysis of **capitalism** and of the political economy practices during his time. Marx bases his work on that of the classical economists like Adam Smith, David Ricardo, and even Benjamin Franklin.

General Theory of Employment, Interest and Money -John Maynard Keynes

The General Theory of Employment, Interest and Money is generally considered to be the masterwork of the English economist John Maynard Keynes. To a great extent, it created the terminology of **modern macroeconomics**. The book ushered in a new age of economic thinking, referred to as the "**Keynesian Revolution**."

Bank Regulations

Since the failure of hundreds of banks during the great depression, the **solvency** of commercial banks has become a responsibility of government. **Demand deposits** are insured by agencies of the government so a depositor is protected from losing assets if a bank should fail. Of course, the major objective of banking regulations is to prevent failures. To maintain the integrity of the banking system, federal and state governments have required commercial banks to follow certain rules and regulations. The most important of these requirements is to ensure banks reserve a certain percentage of their demand deposits as a reserve asset, ensuring that banks do not overextend themselves with loans. Today, only transaction deposits are subject to this rule. This regulation protects depositors against bank insolvency, as does the federal government's insurance plans. The Federal Reserve imposes capital guidelines for commercial banks and savings banks, which provide regulations on certain types of loans. These guidelines are risk-based and protect banks from making poor decisions on a borrower's ability to repay the loan.

Savings

Technically, in economic theory, disposable income is either **consumed** or **saved**. The amount left over when goods and services have been purchased by consumers is considered to be savings. Other categories of savings include corporations' retained earnings and a government surplus. The definition of the term *savings* is subject to various interpretations. Individuals who repay loans of any kind rather than consuming the income are really saving. Interest paid on loans is not savings, but must be counted as income by those who receive the interest. A differentiation must be made between saving, which is to increase assets, and savings, which is one element of a person's total net worth. To save is an activity that results in additional net worth as a separate category. Although this may seem to be a differentiation without a difference, the terms have separate meanings in economic analysis and should be understood in economic terms.

Investments

Investment and savings are two sides of the same coin. If a decision is made to save, the opportunity cost of consumption is sacrificed. Savings can be utilized to **reinvest** in land, capital improvements, and equipment. This type of saving increases the total capita and promotes economic expansion. Savings does not automatically equal **investment**, because both of these decisions are made by different entities in an economy and often for different purposes. It is possible to save yet not increase investment, which can result in a decline in demand, which further leads to increased unemployment, reduction in production, and a business cycle that can lead to recession or depression. This has been named the **paradox of thrift**, because saving more would seem to be a positive spur to the economy, while in many cases it is not. However, when investment increases over savings, aggregate demand is stimulated, and the business cycle may turn toward expansion.

Other Meanings of Investment in Aspects of Finance and Economics

Although investment has a technical meaning in economic theory, it has several other definitions that apply to aspects of finance and economics. In everyday language, we speak of investment as a **speculation** for future gain. Common types of investments are stocks, bonds, government securities, mutual funds, insurance policies, commodities, and real estate. Markets exist in many forms for various types of investments. **Formal exchanges** are the rule in security investing, examples including the New York Stock Exchange and the American Stock Exchange. Investments such as stocks and bonds may provide income in interest and dividends and offer the promise of **appreciation**. Less tangible markets exist for countless items, such as coins, stamps, and markets for professional athletes. Trading in **securities** has become much easier through internet buying and selling. Investment clubs are common in society, and colleges and universities allow students to manage funds as part of their training.

Interest Rates

There are several ways to view interest rates in economics. Interest is the cost of using money in formal analysis. It is the cost of using **capital**. Keynes felt that **interest rates** did not affect saving or investment, as had been believed by classical economists. Classical economics taught that interest rates would adjust toward equilibrium and directly influence savings and investment decisions. As in most areas of economics, the **demand** for and the **supply** of money determine interest rates. The rate of interest will fluctuate depending on many economic variables. Finance employs the term *interest rates* to designate a charge for borrowing money. Interest may also be considered a return on an investment, the interest rate determining the return. It is actually a rate of return on a capital investment. An investor rents money and is charged a percentage of the value of the investment as the cost of borrowing.

Transfer Payments

A transfer payment in economic jargon is any transfer of money from one element of an economy to another, in which there is no expected reciprocal return. Examples of **transfer payments** abound in an economy. Social security transfers, disability and unemployment benefits, and any payment from a government agency for which the recipient does nothing are all forms of transfer payments. Scholarships and interest-free loans are also transfer payments. Transfer payments can also flow between levels of government. Federal disaster relief, subsidies of all kinds, and direct transfers of monies for a multitude of purposes fall into the category of transfer payments. Even state and local taxes are transfer payments in the sense that they are paid by businesses and individuals without getting anything in direct return. Of course, many of the state and municipal functions are providing an indirect return to taxpayers in the form of essential services rendered.

Standard of Deferred Payments

In any transaction, there must be a currency or commodity that is generally accepted as a means of settling debt. **Deferred payment** for a current transaction to be settled later are guided by the standard used at the time. Historically, gold and silver were used as the standard of deferred payments, because they had intrinsic value and everyone could agree on their worth. When the gold standard was in effect, all currencies were guaranteed to be exchanged at a **fixed rate**. In modern economics, the strongest currencies usually serve as the standard of deferred payment. Today, the United States dollar and the European Union's euro are considered the most reliable standard of deferred payment. Illegal transactions rarely allow deferred payments, but if they do, compensation may be made in gold or diamonds, whose store of value is unquestioned. The instability of money at a given time makes the deferred standard of payment more important.

International Monetary Fund

The **international financial network** is a huge and complex array of associations and organizations representing governments, businesses, and individuals. This includes a bewildering number of markets featuring ever-changing exchange rates and fluctuating conditions in the world's economy. Overseeing and monitoring this system is the **International Monetary Fund**. The IMF stands by as a consultant and watchdog over exchange markets and the resulting balance of payments account of participating countries. The IMF is governed by 190 member countries, joining in a cooperative effort to control international markets and avoid financial instability. The institution has grown dramatically since its inception when only 44 countries were included in the charter. Presently, the IMF provides an important role in helping developing nations gain stable economies. Increased membership and the problems of new countries such as those created with the breakup of the Soviet Union have made the role of the IMF an increasingly important one in the world.

Criticisms

As may have been anticipated, the **International Monetary Fund** has become an object of criticism since its charter. One accusation is that the IMF has been partial toward countries that have friendly relations with the United States and other Western powers. Liberal and radical critics accuse the IMF of supporting countries with dictatorships and ignoring complaints regarding civil liberties and human rights in these nations. Defenders of the IMF respond that the organization is an economic group, not a political one. They contend that before a democracy or republic can flourish, it must have a stable economy. The debate continues with liberal politicians supporting the proactive policies of the IMF in stabilizing economies, while more conservative observers feel that supply-side policy would allow the economies of developing nations to grow unimpeded by government intervention. The tendency of the IMF to promote currency devaluation is particularly aggravating to conservative economists and politicians alike.

The World Bank

History

The World Bank was chartered in 1944, when the post-World War II devastation of economies was a major global concern. The organization addressed the problems of rebuilding the economies of Western Europe and providing stability for international investment in those countries (as well as other developing nations). In recent decades, the **World Bank** has become an active participant in reducing poverty and promoting economic growth in **third-world countries**. Included in the economic support is the improvement of education, farming, and manufacturing technology. The major financial tool of the World Bank is to provide funds through **loans** to these countries. The loans usually carry a much lower interest rate than what normally would be charged. The World Bank is actually an association of five separate but related agencies working toward a common goal. It is highly regarded as an organization of integrity by economists and governments alike.

Goals

The work of the World Bank is to provide financial and consulting support for **developing countries**. The problems of dire poverty and famine are common in these countries, and the World Bank is active in attempting to solve these problems. It's tools are primarily financial, but the World Bank serves as an economic resource for financial planning for these countries. Funds are loaned at preferable interest rates to build or repair infrastructure of countries, as well as promote social and economic reforms. Environmental issues are important to the World Bank in making loans and supporting third-world countries. A new emphasis on reducing poverty has influenced recent policy at the World Bank. This includes the advocacy for individual businesses to rebuild flagging economies. Broader goals have been related to the improvement of the standard of living through the promotion of reduced pollution, education, and the creation of entities capable of sustainable growth over time.

Criticisms

Although the World Bank has a generally good reputation in global economics, it is not without its critics. The crux of these concerns is that many of their programs include provisions that alter the structure of the society and rob it of its **autonomy**. Almost always, the World Bank promotes economic liberation from archaic practices, which are sometimes deeply ingrained in the society of a country. These policies often reduce the power of a nation in managing its own economy, in the interest of promoting the general welfare.

Another related criticism of the World Bank is its liberal and progressive political stance. The Bank often requires countries to accept certain conditions as a requisite for financial aid. Sometimes, critics argue that these requirements include reforms not appropriate for unstable governments and countries in conflict. The influence of the United States is often thought to be excessive, and this causes policy that would favor American economic and political interests. Examples include the introduction of foreign businesses to compete with local industries.

Problems with Equating GDP Per Capita and Economic Well-Being

Several economic factors may interfere with equating GDP per capita with individual well-being. A significant allocation of assets is used to combat the negative effects of economic growth such as the destruction of natural habitats and air and water pollution. Economic growth increases such **intangibles** as the increase in commuting, which affects quality of life. Perhaps most importantly, GDP does not account for a significant amount of **domestic production,** such as child-raising and homemaking. The money equivalents for these tasks are omitted from the GDP calculation. There are numerous markets that are left out of GDP, including black markets, criminal activity, and alternative economies. There is also no provision in GDP for volunteer activity, "do it yourself" tasks such as home improvements and landscape management. All of these economic activities are omitted from the formal measurement of per capita GDP and fail to give an accurate picture of individual well-being.

Unemployment in Capitalism

Unemployment in a free market situation occurs only in **capitalistic** economic systems. In Fascism, Socialism, and Communism, the factors of production, including labor, are under the direct control of the **state**. Historically, precapitalist societies such as feudalism formed the basis for the economy. In this case, the serfs were all employed (if able) by mandate of the lords. More primitive societies such as tribes view the entire group as part of one family and take responsibility for ensuring all are cared for adequately. Debate continues on the necessary and appropriate action of governments in curbing unemployment. Liberal and welfare economists often call for a more active role for government in increasing employment, while more conservative analysts feel government intervention exacerbates the problem by its interference. Laws forbidding strikes and layoffs are cited as inappropriate government action to solve unemployment.

Economic Indicators

Business or economic indicators are specific measurements that are used to predict the future course of the economy. They are used as analytical tools to measure and forecast economic activity and future behavior of the economy. Common **economic indicators** are indexes, compilations of data, summaries of economic activity in a period of time, and statistics measuring the level of consumption, investment, savings, and unemployment in the economy. Fluctuations in the money supply and industrial output are important indicators. Measurements for inflation, retail sales, and stock market prices provide supporting data. The National Bureau of Economic Research, whose prime interest is in predicting business cycles, provides many of the important economic indicators used for forecasting. When an indicator occurs behind economic activity, it is called a **lagging indicator**. Indicators current with economic activity are known as **coincident indicators**.

Economic Policy Goals and Tools

Governments and economies usually set **goals** for their economic plans and policy decisions. Goals may be short-term or long-term, and they tend to focus on big-picture elements such as inflation control, employment levels, and economic growth rates. These policy goals are implemented with economic tools that include monetary and fiscal policy, increases or decreases in government spending, international trade practices, regulation of labor markets, and many additional methods.

Often, goals are not exclusively economic, as with defense and other areas of the general welfare. A government must determine which short-term goals are most important to its policy. It may be impossible to reduce inflation while promoting more employment at the same time. Governments are usually more successful with a few short-term goals that work with each other to affect long-term goals. A consistent policy approach to economic problems is essential to achieve economic goals.

Chapter Quiz

Ready to see how well you retained what you just read? Scan the QR code to go directly to the chapter quiz interface for this study guide. If you're using a computer, simply visit the online resources page at **mometrix.com/resources719/apmacroeconom** and click the Chapter Quizzes link.

Macroeconomics

Microeconomics and Macroeconomics

While microeconomics studies the individual units of economic activity, **macroeconomics** takes a larger view. It is the analysis of the **aggregate** of all the economic actions of individuals, corporations, and businesses. This expanded scope includes the issues of government policies to influence the economy. Such national goals include suppressing inflation, stimulating the economy through monetary and fiscal policies, and attaining a maximum employment level. The conduct and regulation of international trade is another area of national interest. There are multiple economic schools of thought that influence macroeconomics. Macroeconomics is an area of continuing evolution, and various tools of economic analysis are used from a variety of sources. The goal of all such schools is to provide the most current and precise economic data and analysis available. Pieces of research carried out by different patterns of economic thinking are combined to produce the most useful and accurate information.

Review Video: Microeconomics and Macroeconomics
Visit mometrix.com/academy and enter code: 538837

Analytical Approaches in Macroeconomics

The two broad divisions of economic analysis are **Keynesian theory**, developed in the 20th century by the English economist John Maynard Keynes, and **supply-side economics**, a current favorite of more conservative economists. Keynesian economics proposes government action to stimulate demand in an economy. Supply-side economics is concerned with the policies that will encourage increased supply by manufacturers and other business organizations. Keynes believed that aggregate demand was the key to understanding fluctuations in the economy. He argued for strong government interventions to attain these goals. Much of the New Deal economics applied during the depression of the 1930s was based on Keynes' theories. The so-called "supply-siders" emphasize the role of the aggregate money supply and fiscal action (or inaction) as the crucial factors in economic growth.

Modern Schools of Macroeconomics

Milton Friedman, a University of Chicago economist, was the chief proponent of **monetarism**, which states that the supply of money in an economy is the major determinant of economic growth or deflation. It eschews the manipulation of aggregate demand in favor of monetary policy that controls the amount of money available in an economy. **Keynesian economics** encourages the proactive role of the government in stimulating aggregate demand to promote economic growth. An offshoot of this school is **New Keynesian economics**, which combines traditional Keynesian theory with microeconomic tools in order to spur demand.

The **Post-Keynesian theorists** incorporate much of Keynesian economics but believe historical patterns in economics lead to more uncertainty in applying economic stimuli to promote demand. **New classical economics** adds the concept of rational expectations to the Keynesian mix. **Austrian economics** is a conservative school that believes the government's activity in economic policy leads to fluctuations in the business cycles.

Milton Friedman

The strongest advocate of the monetary school of macroeconomics was Milton Friedman, an American economist whose theories have become associated with minimal government intervention except in the regulation of the money supply. A Nobel Prize winner in 1976, Friedman's work has included the analysis of **consumption**, as well as an emphasis on **monetary theory and policy**. Friedman has become an icon of conservative economists and politicians for his stance against government spending to spur the economy. Friedman believed that inflation is a direct result of an increase in the money supply and that monetary policy is the most effective tool in managing an economic system. His rejection of government's proactive role in increasing aggregate demand is controversial because it goes against the major themes of government activity of the last 70 years. He argued against many of the Keynesian interventions that have become part of contemporary economics.

Scope of Political Economy

The economic activity and policy of the state are major concerns of **political economy**. Questions such as the level of unemployment, budget surpluses or deficits, and general economic well-being are all important concepts in political economy. Political economy may be said to include all methods of production and distribution of excess funds or remedy of deficits in an economy. The importance of structural relationships in a society is the basis of political economy. The field of general economics places more importance on the allocation of scarce resources to satisfy unlimited demand. Political economy, because it includes social and political elements, is a broader field in a sense. The historical role of a country is very important in political economy. For example, the history of serfdom in Russia set the stage for communism in the early part of the 20th century. American self-reliance and independence set a framework for capitalism to prosper. These historical precedents must be included in the study of political economy.

Balance of Payments

The net sum of a country's exports and imports is known as the **balance of payments** for a country. These trade activities include finished products, raw materials, financial resources, and transfer payments. If the sum total of cash and liquid assets flowing into a country is greater than the outflow, the country has a **positive balance of payments**. If the opposite is the case, the country has a **negative balance of payments. International accounts** include current accounts derived from the net flow of assets resulting from the trade of goods, services, and transfer payments. The accounting of funds received from sales and purchases of financial instruments is called a country's **capital account**. The **foreign reserves account** includes international funds, gold, and balances in exchange accounts. The sum of all these accounts determines the balance of payments for a country.

Monetary System

As in other markets, the same elements of analysis may be used for the **money market**. The laws of demand and supply apply to the money market and result in market equilibrium for the price of money. The quantity of money in the system is also a product of these forces. Money in circulation includes actual paper money and coins. Paper money may be banknotes or Federal Reserve notes that are physically produced by the United State's mint but represent money created by the Federal Reserve based on the credit of the federal government. This credit is electronically created by the government to influence the economy. In reality, since all paper money is based on the promise of the government to honor the currency, all notes are electronically produced. Coins may be produced outside of the Federal Reserve system by legislation. The total money supply is within the scope of the **Federal Reserve System**.

The **money supply** may be measured in a number of ways. Technically, money may be defined as anything that is used to pay a debt, but in practice, money is defined as the currency and coins in circulation. Economic analysis of money uses symbols to designate different measurements of money. The widest definition of money is as "a store of value." In the United States, the Federal Reserve designates the definitions of money measured by various computations. The total of all coins and notes in circulation at any given time is designated by the notation **M0**. **M1:M0** represents all funds in circulation plus all checking and savings accounts (demand deposits). **M2** adds to this money market funds and certificates of deposit held by all investors. These definitions are helpful in monetary analysis by designating components of the money supply in various measurements.

Monetary Exchange Equation and the Current Money Supply

One of the most widely used monetary analytical tools is the **money exchange equation** which provides a link between the money supply and inflation or deflation. Elements of the money exchange equation are the **velocity of money**, defined as the number of times money turns over; the **Gross Domestic Product** (value of all goods and services produced in a period); and the **Gross Domestic Product Deflator**, a measure of inflation in the economy. For instance, M1 in the United States in 2010 was over $1.8 trillion and then over $6.7 trillion in 2020. The M2 figure for the country was over $8.8 trillion in 2010 and then over $19.3 trillion by the end of 2020.

Creation of Money

The total money supply can only be increased (with the exception of coinage) by banks creating new funds through the Federal Reserve System's **electronic crediting process**, where notes are exchanged for electronic credits. The broader definitions of the money supply include demand deposits or checking and savings accounts, plus certificates of deposit. Banks list **demand deposits** as their major assets. A fraction of these deposits may be loaned, thus creating "new" money. That process may be repeated a number of times to expand the money supply. The Federal Reserve controls the amount of new money that can be created by setting a minimum reserve requirement for banks to hold against their total demand deposits. Raising the reserve requirement limits the amount of new money that can be created, while lowering the reserve requirement allows for an expansion of the money supply.

Function of Bank Reserves at the Central Bank

To create additional funds in the money supply, the **central bank** (The Federal Reserve in the United States) may buy a quantity of government securities on the open market, thus increasing money available for banks to lend out under the fractional reserve system. This will increase the total money supply. To reduce the money supply, the central bank sells government securities on the open market and depletes the funds in the private banks. In this manner, the Federal Reserve maintains some control over the total money in circulation. **Private banks**, in turn, loan out a percentage of the funds, which, in effect, creates new money. The funds may then be turned over or multiplied many times, increasing the impact of the initial increase in money.

Money Market Instruments

There are a variety of money market securities or instruments available for trading. A common type is a draft or bill drawn on a bank, which guarantees full payment of the amount. This is known as a "**banker's acceptance**." Promissory notes or drafts have a specific maturity date and are sold at a discount on the open market. Time deposits with specific maturity dates and a specified rate of interest are known as **certificates of deposit**. Short-term government securities such as **Treasury Bills** are issued by various federal or quasi-federal agencies. Federal securities include deposits held by the Federal Reserve at any of their branches or agencies. These notes all carry an interest charge. Cities, towns, and counties often float short-term issues to finance specific projects or general operations. Treasury Bills are very short-term securities issued by the Federal government and are traded on the open market.

CURRENCY

Currency may be defined technically as any legal tender with which debts may be settled. **Currency's** major use is to facilitate the exchange of goods and services in the marketplace. The world is divided into "currency zones" that determine what currency may be used in trade. Rates of exchange are a market where different currencies may be bought and sold. Both banknotes and coins are considered currency. The country that issues the currency owns a **monopoly** in that market. Central banks of countries are the institutions that control currency (and the money supply) through monetary and fiscal policy. These central banks or other monetary authorities (set up as an agency by the government) control and implement monetary policy and activity. Such authorities differ in their power from country to country. For example, in the United States, the Federal Reserve is a wholly independent agency free of political controls. Although Congress legislated the Federal Reserve into existence, it remains completely independent in its activity.

GOLD STANDARD

A monetary system linked to the value of gold is said to be on the **gold standard**. Those who issue currency agree to exchange banknotes and coins for gold based on a fixed exchange rate. Thus, gold becomes the basic unit of account to measure all wealth against. Gold standards were created to stabilize currencies by making it impossible for governments to create money at their pleasure. The gold standard also protects against hyperinflation and the overexpansion of debt in an economy. Originally, when the major form of money was coins (usually silver or gold) there was a logic to the gold standard. The gold standard was once a common phenomenon among nations but has now been replaced by systems giving the central banks of countries the power to create money and manipulate monetary policy for the good of the economy. No modern country would return to the gold standard despite the protection it affords.

HISTORICAL USE OF GOLD AS STORE OF VALUE

Gold was historically considered to be the ideal measure of wealth and a practical unit of account for market transactions. **Gold** was rare, easily measured and divided (originally by weight), extremely durable, and provided a uniform measure of value that transcended geographical boundaries, making it ideal for settling debts between nations or individuals living in different areas. Gold may be easily transported and was used as a convenient base for the early banking systems in the world. Banknotes and other forms of paper currencies have obvious practical advantages over gold. Besides providing central banks with the power to create money, paper currencies are portable and resistant to hoarding,. The complexity of the world economy made gold obsolete in the modern world except as an investment or reserve. International trade in the modern world could not be conducted with gold as the measure of value.

THEORY OF THE GOLD STANDARD

The **central rationale** for the gold standard is the theory that an increase in the money supply will cause inflation. If there is speculation over the value of money in the future, **uncertainty** will erode economic growth. Such uncertainty about the true value of money leads to a chaotic economy. The gold standard was implemented in most cases to stem this uncertainty. The gold standard would guarantee confidence in the economy, and benefit both domestic and international commerce. A second reason for instituting the gold standard was to put stringent limits on the role of the central bank in controlling the economy. Governments were thought to be inept in economic affairs, and the gold standard ensured a limit on their participation. The gold standard would also build confidence in money markets and inspire individuals and businesses to boost economic activity without fear of government intervention.

GOLD AS A RESERVE TODAY

Today, gold is held by nations to protect their currencies and provide a stable reserve of stored value in an economy. Gold tends to **fluctuate** with the rise and fall of the dollar on exchange markets. When the dollar depreciates in relation to other currencies, the value of gold rises. Thus, gold serves as a stable financial asset in the portfolios of almost all central banks in the world. It serves a type of **internal reserve** that may be called upon should adverse economic conditions arise. Banks may also use gold as a reserve against loans to their own governments as well as international trading partners. Banks seek to hold in reserve assets with "real value" rather than electronically produced money. They may add real property, silver, and other stable assets to protect themselves. International banks also tend to hold significant amounts of United States dollars because of the stability inherent in the American economy. Central banks must feel they have stable assets to meet any economic crisis that might arise.

INFLATION

Inflation strikes when there is a general price increase of goods and services against one currency. A price index, such as the **Consumer Price Index**, can be used as a measuring tool to compare prices at different times. A fictional "market basket" of commonly consumed staples is measured and charted over a period of time (usually one year). If the price of the representative market basket has gone up, **inflation** has occurred. For example, if a typical basket costs $500 this year as compared to $400 last year for the same basket, inflation has risen over a year. Inflation reduces the buying power of money, and if uncontrolled, can threaten the entire economy. An example of **runaway inflation** occurred in Germany in the 1930s. Inflation was rampant and people had to take large quantities of physical money to markets to exchange for goods and services. This rampant inflation helped bring the Nazis to power. **Deflation**, the general lowering of prices and the subsequent increase in purchasing power of money is a much less frequent phenomena.

MEASUREMENT

Measuring inflation can be an inexact science, because there are a number of price indexes that can be utilized. Most price indexes are based on information gleaned through government agencies and institutions. To accurately **measure the rate of inflation**, hypothetical market baskets of goods are compared from year to year. An adjustment termed a **hedonic adjustment** may be applied if there is a change in the makeup of the basket of goods. The weight given to each product or service in the basket will affect the rate of inflation. The **inflation rate** is the percentage rate of the price increase from one year to the next on identical bundles of goods. The United States has suffered through some significant periods of inflation, particularly after World War II. Europe has been plagued with hyperinflation, which is an extreme rise in prices due to the fall of the purchasing power of money. Such hyperinflation destabilizes economies and may result in political and social crises, as well as an economic one.

Indexes: There are a number of indexes that may be used to chart the rise of inflation. Perhaps the most common one is the **cost-of-living index**, which seeks to measure how much it actually costs an individual to live for a specified period of time. This index is measured by the **Consumer Price Index**, which prices bundles of goods and services and compares them over time. Another reliable measuring tool is the **Producer Price Index**, which accounts for the actual amount of money the producer of goods and services receives. This is a net figure that considers other economic realities such as taxes in the computation. **Commodity price indexes** focus on changes in prices of essential commodities used in an economy. They are widely used in agricultural economics. There are indexes that measure price changes in products sold by wholesalers, which are then passed on to retailers for sale to consumers. Some indexes attempt to pinpoint the personal consumption of individuals, but this is difficult to do with any degree of accuracy.

MISERY INDEX

The "Misery Index" was developed to measure the economic hardships of combined unemployment and inflation. Although controversial, this index attempts to ascertain the level of economic impact on citizens in a society beset with the twin problems of **inflation** and **unemployment**. Economists have not been able to agree on the effect of such an index on individuals or businesses. There is a school of thought that argues that previous histories of inflation linked to economic unhappiness have conditioned the public to regard any increase in inflation to be cause for concern. For example, a relatively low level of rising prices may have a psychological impact beyond the economic one. Some inflation is considered necessary to balance the business cycle during periods of recession. One could say that the public takes a much dimmer view of inflation than do economists. This difference becomes important if the public reacts negatively to minor inflation and it becomes an expectation of a weakened economy.

CAUSES

Pinpointing the **causes** of inflation is an area of controversy. Monetary theory holds that inflation is a direct result of an increase in the money supply without a corresponding growth of the entire economy. In the most simple terms, this means the amount of money available for consumption will be the prime determinant of spending in the economy. Neo-Keynesian economists feel that the injection into the economy of large expenditures by the government and its agencies is a goad to economic growth. They posit the theory of **demand-pull inflation**, where the demand by consumers for goods and services and the inability of the economy to respond to increased demand cause prices to rise. **Cost-push inflation** is the result of a sudden and unexpected increase in the cost of an essential product or service. Some believe that inflation is a permanent feature of a modern economy, where guaranteed wage increases and adaptive economic behavior based on past history ensure some level of inflation will occur regularly in an economy.

STRATEGIES FOR COMBATING INFLATION

Most modern countries are in a constant struggle with **inflation**. There are several strategies employed to keep price increases at an acceptable level. Central banks have the power to fight inflation by applying monetary policy and, most importantly, by setting interest rates. When inflation threatens an economy, the raising of interest rates acts as a deterrent to price increases by making money more costly and slowing the economic activity of a country. Central banks have the autonomy to apply these measures when they feel they are appropriate. An imposition of wage and price controls is a more drastic way to slow or halt inflation. These measures have many drawbacks, including the possibility of depressing the economy too far. Controls also promote hoarding and artificial shortages and sometimes encourage the creation of alternative marketplaces that impair economic growth.

HYPERINFLATION

Runaway, or hyperinflation, is an economic crisis in which prices rise at an alarming rate as currency becomes devalued. There are no accurate measurements for **hyperinflation**, but economists agree a general and rapid raising of prices without a corresponding movement toward equilibrium is a recipe for runaway inflation. True hyperinflation is recognized when governments are forced to dramatically increase the money supply as currency loses value. Most hyperinflation is created by the printing of vast quantities of **paper money** to attempt to react to price increases. This usually initiates a spiral of increasing prices and decreasing value of the currency. This cycle is difficult to break, because expectations of individuals and businesses are for yet more rising prices and devalued money. A common reaction to hyperinflation is the use of hard money as a store of value and medium of exchange.

STAGFLATION

When high inflation is joined by a depressed economy and high unemployment, the result has been called "**stagflation**." Unexpected changes to an aggregate supply can create an economic trauma that has implications for the entire economy. Stagflation creates a dilemma for central banks. If the bank chooses to stimulate the economy by lowering the reserve requirements for commercial banks and reducing the interest rates, it runs the risk of generating too much money, which will increase inflation. Should the bank elect to combat inflation by raising the interest rates and the reserve requirement of banks, these actions could depress the economy further and result in more unemployment. Both choices have significant negative results for a struggling economy. When the United States faced this dilemma in the 1970s, it was thought to have been caused by the failure of the government to gauge prices. The ultimate response to this period of stagflation was the emergence of supply-side economics as a strategic tool. Economists disagree on the effectiveness of this strategy.

QUALITIES OF MONEY

All money or forms of exchange share common characteristics which define the store of value of the currency used. Money must be a generally accepted medium for trading and settling debts. Acceptance of money depends on trust in the **issuing institution or nation**.

To be useful as a deferred payment instrument, money must serve as a basic unit of account in an economic system. This requisite is fulfilled if money is seen to be a **standard of value** through which other goods may be given comparative value. The relative cost of any good or service must be measured against a standard which is the value of money. Perhaps most importantly, money must be accepted as a **store of value** by everyone in an economy. In this manner, money is a representation of the essential worth of any traded good or service. The system of deferred payment under which most markets operate makes it imperative that money has its own essential store of value resting on the promise of a central bank or nation to honor the currency.

EFFECTS OF MONEY IN ECONOMICS

Money is an essential element in economics and forms the basis for individual, business, and government markets. Both the quality and the quantity of money affect the economy in fundamental ways. Central banks manipulate **money quantities** in order to influence the economy by expanding or contracting available funds. **Monetary policies** of nations have an important impact on the economies of those countries. It can be used to stimulate growth or to slow an overheated economy. **Monetary failure** in a economy produces uncertainty and chaotic markets. When the USSR dissolved in the early 1990s, a financial crisis occurred that still impacts some nations. Defining money in the modern world can be difficult due to the myriad of forms of credit available globally. The revolution started by credit cards in the last 50 years has completely changed the nature of exchange in most markets. Money has many substitutes, including demand deposits, savings accounts, and credit and debit cards, which serve as a store of value that is generally accepted.

SHRINKING THE MONEY SUPPLY

Sometimes, monetary policy demands a **reduction** in the quantity of money available in the economy. Central banks have the power to destroy or remove from circulation coins and paper currency at their discretion. Only a small fraction of the total money supply is represented by coins and notes. Money is **destroyed** when government securities are purchased and when debt is paid off or canceled. Buying government bonds or other federal or state notes and paper takes that money out of the system. If a debt is paid to an institution such as a commercial bank, that money is lost from the total supply of funds. The Treasury of the United States is empowered to reduce the money supply through open market operations or retiring government debt. When money is withdrawn from a bank, the money supply is reduced because the bank can no longer loan out the funds and thereby create new money.

Measures of National Income and Output

National income may be defined as the aggregate figure of all consumption, individual, business, and governmental income, plus total investments and the balance of trade accounts for a country. This aggregate number, derived from adding these categories together, is called the **expenditure method** of national income determination. Another calculation to determine the national income is to account for all the goods and services produced in a country during a fixed period. This is called the **production accounting** of national income. Yet another way of computing national income is to total all income received by individuals, businesses, and governments to arrive at total national income. This is the **income approach** to national income accounting. To summarize, there are three ways of calculating national income: total expenditures, total value of production, and the aggregate consumption figures for a country.

GNP

The **Gross National Product** (GNP) is one of the prime indicators of the economic health of a country. Typically, this is an aggregate figure which includes all goods and services **produced** in the economy for a specified period, usually one year. This computation uses "final" goods and services to reach the aggregate production. This means that raw materials produced and sold to manufacturers are not included if they are to be used to make final products that are then sold as final goods. GNP reflects only new final products for the measurement period are counted; markets and transactions in used goods are omitted from GNP. Allocations of GNP are decided by the nation that owns the business unit, not where the goods are sold. For example, funds received from a Volvo manufactured and sold in the United States would be counted as part of Sweden's GNP, as they are the owners of the corporation. This means that all proceeds of sales of final goods belong in the national account of the country that claims ownership of the firm that sold the goods.

GDP

Another important measure of economic health is **Gross Domestic Product** (GDP). This calculation aggregates all goods and services sold in a specified period but allocates monies determined by where the **sale** actually takes place, rather than what country owns the business. A Volvo automobile manufactured and sold in the United States would be included in the GDP of America because it was earned in the United States, even though the business owners are Swedish. It follows that to compute GNP from GDP, the aggregate total of income from goods sold by other countries must be subtracted from GDP. Gross Domestic Product is a strong indicator of the short-term health of an economy as it measures current aggregate production. It is not as reliable a measure for accounting for the sources, and allocations of a country's income. GDP is a better measure of the state of production in the short term. GNP is better when analyzing sources and uses of income.

Gross Value Added, Depreciation, and Net National Product

A significant portion of GNP is reserved and used for refurbishing and maintaining the productive capacity of a country. This includes monies used to repair and replace capital equipment that has become obsolete or inefficient. This total **depreciation** is the amount of GNP reserved for the replacement and service of capital goods. The **national income approach** is a calculation of the total income earned in a period, minus depreciation, indirect taxes, and direct taxes. **Personal income**, a major component of the income method, is the net national income minus taxes, retained earnings, and transfer payments by governments. **Personal disposable income**, the amount of income available for consumption is the total personal income minus personal taxes and plus transfer payments. It is useful for economists to break down categories in order to analyze the interactions and relationships between elements of income earned in a country.

National Income and Welfare

There are many ways to measure the **welfare** of an individual in an economy. Although non-economic issues affect welfare to a large degree, economic welfare can be measured mathematically. Dividing the total net disposable income by the total population gives an economic value to welfare. Using economic value as an indicator, there is a correlation between this figure and various other measures of welfare. Some problems exist in any attempt to measure actual **disposable income**. There is a significant amount of unpaid economic activity, including domestic functions such as the care of children. Mothers who are "employed" in childcare and running homes are not included in national income, which is an obvious flaw in the calculation. Other factors important to welfare are the quality of life, which includes social well-being; freedom from ecological pollution; and political and religious choice. These factors are only indirectly measured in the welfare of individuals in a society.

Real and Nominal Values

In the analysis of GNP, there are inherent problems. Due to the presence of inflation, price levels rise virtually every year, leading to a rise in "nominal" increase in GNP, even if there is no increase in production or income. This gives an unrealistic picture of GNP and paints an optimistic picture that is not entirely accurate. This figure is called **"nominal" GNP**. **Real GNP** is the nominal figure adjusted for inflation. If inflation is five percent, this figure must be applied to the total income or production figures to find real value. An accurate computation of GNP must compare gross figures of income or production for two periods by designating values of goods and services after inflation. This real GNP is a much more accurate measurement of the growth and health of an economy. The higher the rate of inflation the larger the differential between nominal and real national income.

Wealth

The definition of wealth is both an objective and subjective one. In common usage, **wealth** is understood to consist primarily of money, land, and investments of an individual. However, wealth includes many subjective factors that cannot be measured by strictly economic values. Additionally, concepts of wealth differ between cultures and societies. **Economic wealth** must be measured in relation to all other individuals in the same economic systems. The income of a middle-class American would make a third-world citizen very wealthy. Within the United States, cost-of-living, income, and taxes vary widely. A wealthy person in Iowa may not be considered wealthy in Los Angeles because of differences in the economic situations of the two places. Additionally, intangibles such as environmental health, health of the individual, quality of life, and dozens of other less objective factors all must be accounted for in considering **real wealth**.

Monetary Policy

The managing of the economy by manipulating and adjusting the money supply is called **monetary policy**. Usually addressing specific goals, monetary policy includes adjusting prime interest rates, buying or selling government securities in open market operations, and setting reserve requirements for commercial banks. The higher the reserve requirement, the less funds are available for expansion of the money supply. Two major elements are in play in monetary policy: the **amount** of money in the economy and the level of **interest rates** (the cost of using money). Monetary policy is geared to affect each of these variables in order to influence the economy. Monetary policy may be easy, with lower interest rates and reserve requirements, or tighter, with higher interest rates and higher reserve requirements. Monetary policy as an economic policy is favored by more conservative economists and politicians, while more liberal analysts prefer Keynesian methods stimulating aggregate demand.

History

The use of **monetary policy** as a major factor in influencing the economy is a fairly recent phenomenon, beginning in the 18th century and becoming a common strategy since the 1950s. Originally, monetary policy concerned itself with increasing or decreasing the supply of money in the economy. Now, much more sophisticated methods involving a bevy of financial tools and types of interventions. Monetary policy in its broadest sense includes both long- and short-term interest rates, the quality and quantity of credit available, and the purchase and sale of government securities. It seeks to deter government action to influence aggregate demand through injections of money into the economy. Monetary policy also influences exchange rates, the velocity of money in the economy, and the ownership of securities in the economy. The most extreme position on monetary policy is a return to the gold standard. This is a minority position held by only a few fringe economists. To adopt the gold standard would severely limit other tools of monetary policy.

Trends in Central Banking

As monetary policy has become more proactive in modern economies, more sophisticated tools have been employed to **influence the economy**. The monetary level could be changed only by relatively crude methods, particularly when the gold standard was in place. Now, central banks are active in the sale and purchase of **government long- and short-term securities**, which provides a tool for expansion or contraction of the money supply. Selling government securities takes money out of the supply, while buying these instruments injects new money into the system. The other method used effectively by monetary policy is **changing the reserve requirements** for commercial banks. An increase in the reserve requirement contracts the supply of money by compelling banks to keep a higher percentage of demand deposits. A reduction of the reserve requirement allows commercial banks to lend out more funds, increasing the money supply. Interest rates may also be lowered on secured loans to banks. If the rate is lowered enough, commercial banks will borrow from the central bank and loan out these funds in turn.

Inflation Targeting

Monetary policy may be used as a tool to limit **inflation**. This goal is attained by **raising the rate of interest**, which tends to restrain economic growth and tighten money. The Federal Reserve chairman announces periodic reviews and incremental adjustments to the interest rates as deemed necessary for the health of the economy. When the rate of interest is raised, it will cost commercial banks more to borrow from the central bank, thus cooling the economy. Although the interest rates are determined by an independent agency, they are subject to both social and political influence. In the United States, a committee of the Federal Reserve Bank monitors and adjusts interest rates. Close attention is given to the economic information that indicates inflation is rising, falling, or steady. A defined goal of the central bank is to control inflation; therefore, monitoring indicators in the economy is an ongoing task. The chairman of the Federal Reserve has become a familiar public figure due to multiple appearances before Congress to give reports on the state of the economy.

Federal Reserve and Creation of Money

An example of how money is **created** may be understood by following the flow of funds. Suppose someone deposits $100 in his or her commercial bank. Assuming a reserve requirement of 10%, the commercial bank creates more money by lending $90 to a qualified borrower. This increases the money supply by $190. The additional money may be used for consumption, savings, or investment. A second example would be the purchase of government securities. If commercial paper is purchased from an individual for $100, that individual has an extra $100 to consume, save, or invest. In any case, the amount of money in circulation has increased by $100. When the Federal Reserve lowers interest rates, both businesses and individuals are encouraged to borrow and consume. This tool has far-reaching effects in managing the economy.

Criticisms of Monetary Policy

Some schools of economics that favor markets free of government "interference" object to any monetary policy as a distortion of the marketplace. The so-called **Austrian school of economics** vehemently opposes monetary policy in any form. Advocates of market freedom argue that the "invisible hand" of self-interest should determine economic activity. In a situation of a free market, consumers will decide, based on their perceived self-interest, whether to consume goods now or at a later time. This is referred to as a saver's "**time presence**." Consumption now would deplete savings and cause a rise in interest rates due to the increased demand for money. Deferring consumption lowers the interest rate by reducing the demand for money. Critics of monetary policy say that such policies do not accurately reflect consumers' preferences, as they are artificially manipulated. When consumer preferences are ignored, businesses will often mistake lowered rates with consumer confidence and make poor investment choices.

National Income and Product Accounts

The accounting for national income uses traditional accounting procedures to report the state of the economy measured by aggregate income. Both businesses and government resources are used to prepare the reports. Typically, double-entry bookkeeping practices are used in recording the economic information. The left side of the report lists all earned income for the period, with salaries and wages being the most dominant numbers in the account. The right side of the report summarizes production information, including consumption, investment, savings, transfer payments, and net exports (balance of trade). Totals for the two sides must be the same when all economic factors are considered. **National income** represents the total income of employees, government income, rental income, corporate income, and the net balance of transfer payments. Each of these categories is subject to specific defining qualities to ensure the accounts are accurate.

Economic Growth

Although there are many ways to measure **economic growth**, the increase of the store of value is a common rule used in macroeconomic analysis. It may be understood as the aggregate wealth of an economic entity. A common calculation used to determine economic growth is to measure the aggregate value of all goods and services that an economy produces. A true measurement of economic growth must discount inflation to be an accurate evaluation. This is called **real-time measurement**. In formal economic analysis, economic growth is determined by the total production of an economy adjusted for price rises. Economists often use GDP to evaluate growth. Per capita GDP may indicate the level of the well-being of an individual in an economy. Per capita GDP does not account for all the factors that determine the well-being of people in an economy.

"Limits to Growth" Debate

Economic growth carries with it substantial costs, both measurable and intangible. Given a world of limited resources, economic growth includes the more rapid **depletion** of such resources. The combined effects of economic growth on air and water pollution are too great to be measured. The destruction of rainforests and extinction of plant and animal species at an unprecedented rate are added, and sometimes hidden, costs of economic growth. The combination of rapid growth and resource depletion may eventually **stop economic growth** completely. The introduction of new technology has fueled the rate of economic growth in the world. This technology may also be able to allow growth without many of the negative results. Many social scientists and economists contend growth must slow or stop in order to maintain a level of well-being that is acceptable. Others put faith in the ability of mankind to innovate and adjust to allow growth without devastating consequences.

Good and Bad Economic Growth

Often, economists involved in analysis and policy decisions work on the assumption that all growth is good, without regard to the social costs. From a strict economic perspective, almost all economic growth may be rationalized as worthwhile. Using these precepts, plans and policies that are damaging to the general welfare may be defended effectively. For example, opening natural habitats for exploration of fossil fuels seems to make economic sense given the demand for oil. The costs of such decisions is not always readily apparent, but over time degrades the quality of life. **Positive economic growth** involves the consideration of social and environmental factors in making economic policy. A successful economy does little good if the quality of life declines as a result of the growth. Economies exist for and because of the people and social systems they serve. If they fail to improve the general welfare, they have failed regardless of economic growth.

Purchasing Power Parity

In international trade or speculation in currency markets, there must be a tool that uses a common measurement to compare value. This tool is called **purchasing power parity**, which provides an estimate of the number of goods and services that can be purchased with different currencies. This tool is handy for understanding comparative value and measuring living standards in different countries. Differences in income levels in countries and fluctuations in price levels make purchasing power parity an important analytical tool when comparing the value of currencies. In international trade, it is imperative to know the equivalent value of the two countries trading so that each buyer and seller understands the purchasing power of the monies involved. Differences in prices, standard of living, production, and consumption variables are considered in the purchasing power parity calculation. This avoids complex analyses of independent variables in each country.

Rational Expectations

In macroeconomics, the concept of **rational expectations** is used to provide a model of the results of economic decisions. The theory of rational expectations was first posited in the early 1960s as a refined tool for understanding the results of proposed economic actions. This theory has proved exceptionally useful in evaluating macroeconomic trends in **Keynesian economic theory**. For example, a business may wish to make a pricing change in a product and needs to know how this would affect sales and income. The rational expectations model would project the impact of the price change on the business. In a sense, rational expectations are an informed guess after considering all available economic information. The theory cannot make predictions about human behavior in the marketplace without assumptions to provide a frame of reference. Outcomes that are forecast using this model do not differ significantly from the state of market equilibrium. Rational expectation models form the foundations of **efficient markets theory**.

Unemployment

In economics, an **unemployed** person is one who has the will and capacity to work, but cannot find meaningful employment. The total number of unemployed people as a ratio to the entire labor pool is the **rate of unemployment**. The measurement of people without jobs who are actively seeking work is very difficult to determine. A number of methods for measuring unemployment are used, each with its own flaws and advantages. The comparison of unemployment between different countries is very inaccurate due to different definitions of unemployment and different social structures of countries. Unemployment has significant costs to both an economy and society but also provides some economic benefits. Depending on the perspective taken, unemployment at various levels will affect an economy in different ways. More conservative economists argue that the marketplace will determine unemployment, while welfare economists call for government action in the field.

Costs

Unemployment has both **social and economic costs** to individuals and society. The psychological impact of being unemployed degrades self-esteem, creates a sense of purposelessness, and increases mental strain. The financial implications can impair family life, reduce the standard of living, and make it difficult for some to receive benefits such as health insurance and disability payments, which are often part of an employment package. When workers are unable to find appropriate positions for their level of training and education, they are sometimes forced to take inferior jobs. These individuals are said to be underemployed and are generally dissatisfied members of the workforce. High unemployment has profound economic costs in many situations. It typically reflects low GDP, which implies both inefficient use of resources and the failure of production to provide products that improve the general welfare.

Benefits

The major benefit of unemployment is that it has a **"cooling" effect** on the economy and tends to **restrict general inflation**. Many economists feel that given the scarcity of natural resources and the environmental pollution associated with rapid economic growth, it is not possible to continue increasing GDP year after year. Unemployment is a restraint to such growth. Welfare economists argue the burdens of slowing the economy should not fall on the poorest and least able to cope members of society. They believe improved technology and planned economic growth that considers environmental factors will allow modest, healthy growth with low unemployment. In any economy, there are a certain number of members of the workforce moving from job to job and seeking work they consider more appropriate to their skills. This common type of unemployment is termed **frictional unemployment**.

Types

There are several types of unemployment recognized by economists. **Cyclical unemployment** results in recessionary periods of the business cycle when aggregate demand falls. When there is a major change in structure or skill level of an industry, unemployment may result. The advent of computers for word processing made typewriters virtually obsolete, causing those who make, sell, and repair typewriters to be unemployed. Changes in the market due to shifting demand for certain products affect the employees who produce those goods. If demand for typewriters falls, demand for the labor involved with typewriter production and sale also drops. This is also an example of unemployment caused by **technological advances**. Another type of unemployment is **seasonal unemployment**, where productive activity in an industry is limited to certain times of the year. Commercial harvesting of oysters is such a seasonal position.

Measurement in the United States

Measuring unemployment in the United States is done with statistics and data obtained by the **US Bureau of Labor Statistics**. Most countries have a similar agency providing this service. The major criterion for determining if an individual was gainfully employed during the weekly measuring period is straightforward. People are deemed to have been employed if they did any activity for pay or profit during the period. Included in this group are temporary workers and seasonal employees. Included in this calculation of employment are those who do hold jobs but were unable to work because of personal obligations, holidays, sickness, labor strikes or lock-outs, inclement weather, or temporary maternity or paternity reasons. Homemakers, students, and those imprisoned are excluded from the calculation of the employed. Individuals are classified as unemployed if they have actively sought work in the previous month and are ready and able to be employed.

Recessions

The technical definition of a **recession** is when a nation's real Gross Domestic Product decreases in two or more consecutive quarters of the fiscal year. Typically, recessions involve falling aggregate demand, which causes prices to fall and economic activity to slow. It sometimes occurs when inflation rises quickly and is combined with a slowing economy. This condition is called "**stagflation**." In general, recessions are characterized by falling prices. Recessions appear in a more or less regular pattern in capitalistic economies. Recent patterns have indicated a recession may be expected every five to ten years. Most recessions are caused by lack of consumer and business confidence in the future. Some economists encourage government intervention in a recession, while others feel such interference only adds to the problem. The latter group are more conservative economists who prefer to let the market determine the level of economic activity.

Depression in the United States

Only once has the United States gone through a massive **depression**. In the 1920s, massive speculation and investment in stocks caused their prices to rise far above their true value. Adding to the problem was the fact that many of the stocks were purchased on credit, using securities as collateral. When the economy began to contract, share prices fell dramatically and the collateral supporting other stock purchases became worthless. The loans were called, became uncollectible, and triggered a financial panic that led to multiple failures in the banking system. Savings were lost, unemployment soared, and the economy spiraled into a depression. After the election of **Franklin Roosevelt** in 1932, large amounts of money were injected into the economy. Precautions against future bank failures were addressed by federal insurance programs, and speculation in the stock market was regulated as well. Although these measures helped the economy, it was not until the United States entered World War II that it emerged from the effects of the depression.

Multiplier Effect

The multiplier effect is a theory that postulates that a single injection of funds into an economy may cause an effect far beyond what might be anticipated. The **multiplier effect** is an analytical tool favored by Keynesian economists to advance their theories of increasing aggregate demand. For example, a decision to build a new shopping center has a much bigger impact on the economy than indicated in the single transaction. Builders will be hired, retail stores will open, and restaurants and theatres may flourish, all creating jobs and income that far outweigh the initial investment in the shopping center. The multiplier effect is seen most clearly in economic situations where there are significant unused resources in the economy that may be engaged by an investment of capital. This investment is said to increase incomes, demand, and employment and give a general boost to the economy. Not all schools of economics recognize the multiplier effect equally, but it has become a standard tool in modern economics.

Accelerator Effect

The accelerator effect is a hypothetical theory that posits that the general economic condition will have a major impact on **private investment** in the economy. The sequence of events may occur as follows: as Gross Domestic Product rises, business confidence increases with the expectation of increasing sales, income, profit, and more efficient use of existing resources. The expansion spiral may continue as businesses increase investment and employment, and worker income and consumption also rise. The multiplier effect can accelerate all of these economic indicators, causing yet more expansion. The accelerator effect may also be seen in a contracting economy. As economic activity slows, businesses cut employment and investment in anticipation of reduced profits. These effects are all accelerated and the downward spiral of the economy is exacerbated. If unchecked, this deflationary spiral may lead to a **recession**, or in the worst case, a **depression**.

Economic Cycles

Cycles of expansion and contraction of economic activity seen regularly in economies are called **business (or economic) cycles**. The expansion or contraction tends to occur across the board in almost all areas of economic activity, contributing to the impact and intensified by the accelerator concept. Standard measurements of economic activity are increases or decreases in the **real Gross Domestic Product**. Although there are definite patterns of economic cycles, they cannot be predicted accurately because of multiple factors affecting the economy. Cycles tend to have their own lifespan, and there is a debate as to whether government interventions are useful in smoothing out the fluctuations. The **prediction of economic cycles** has become a major factor in business, social, and political arenas.

Green Economics

Green economics is a general term that includes economics as one part of the total ecological system. It is an interdisciplinary branch of economics, including contributions from the social sciences, biology, and economics. **Green economics** should be thought of as a loose confederation of movements, ideas, schools, and theorists, rather than a single solid school of thought. A general mission statement for green economics is that the economy is one element in the **ecosystem**, and the ecosystem plays an important role in economic decisions. The concept of scarce resources is central to green economics, as is the idea of sustainable resources. Given the agreement that all resources are limited in a sense, green economics advocates moderate economic growth, with ecologically sound principles that maintain rather than consume our limited resources.

Government Debt in Depth

Any obligation owed by local, state, or federal governments is considered **government debt**. Such a debt is actually an indirect debt of the taxpayers as a whole, though it is seldom understood this way. Debt is most often incurred by issuing securities, primarily bonds, with varying lengths of maturity. Debt that is owed to citizens of the country incurring the obligation, is known as **internal debt**. However, debt held by individuals, institutions, and governments from another country is called **external debt**. Although the great majority of government debt is incurred by notes and bonds, some governments may borrow from central or commercial banks. Fiscal conservatives rail against public debt while more liberal economists and politicians support raising funds for social welfare and defense. The issue of United States public debt, also called the **deficit**, has become an issue in politics and welfare economics.

Economic Models

In economics, as in other disciplines, **models** are constructed simulations of actual problems in order to test a set of variables. Models provide a framework that clearly illustrates the change in economic elements when different variables are applied. In economics, a model is a theoretical construct that represents economic processes by a set of variables and a set of logical and quantitative relationships between them. As in other fields, models are simplified frameworks designed to illuminate complex processes. Economic models are widely used in academic settings and in economic research. Businesses use economic models to plan and allocate resources, as well as predict the impact of economic actions. Governments use models of the economy to plan policies and justify the implementation of economic decisions. Models are also useful in predicting future economic activity.

Econometrics

A collection of mathematical and statistical tools used in advanced economic theory are given the general name of **econometrics**. Econometrics is used extensively in economic research and in the creation of economic models. Econometrics allows researchers to place numerical values on economic concepts and verify posited hypotheses. An example of a widely used econometric formula is regression analysis. When econometrics is used to study a variable over a specified span of time it is referred to as a **time-series analysis**. An example would be the impact of savings in a business cycle for the past 30 years. When econometrics is employed to measure different variables at one point in time, it is termed **cross-sectional analysis**. Both time-series and cross-sectional analyses are used extensively in economic modeling.

Definitions Used for Macroeconomics of the Labor Market

Macroeconomics of the labor market starts with a series of definitions calculated from labor statistics:

- The **labor force** includes all people in an economy who have jobs or are actively seeking employment.
- To find the **participation rate** of individuals in the workforce, the aggregate number of the labor pool is divided by the size of the total population.
- The **unemployment rate** is calculated as a percentage of those who are unemployed but seeking jobs relative to the total population.

From these basic definitions, we can obtain **stock variables**, which measure a level at a particular point in time. **Flow variables**, on the other hand, are used to measure a variable over a specified period of time. Examples of flow variables include modifications of the labor market due to net entries and exits from the labor pool. This would include retirees, net immigration of eligible laborers, forced unemployment, and frictional unemployment. These are flow variables that may be studied over any length of time.

Balance of Payments

The measurement of a nation's **trade productivity** is the net of the imports and exports of finances, services, and finished goods in international trade with other countries. Financial capital and transfer payments also enter into the calculation. Each country has three accounts to measure international trade activity. The **current account** of a country has three components: the transfer account (for unilateral transfers), the income account (measuring net income received from international transactions), and the trade account (a record of goods and survives traded abroad). The **capital account** indicates the net gain or loss in capital obtained from international trade. This is primarily used for cash and financial paper, including loans, investments, and savings. Finally, the **unilateral transfer account** notes all transfers of asset for which there is no compensation. Each account may either have a surplus indicating the country gained more than they lost in that account, or a deficit noting the net loss for the country. The net total of all accounts gives a balance of payments figure for that period.

Okun's Law

Arthur Okun, an American economist, noted that changing unemployment rates had a significant impact on real GDP. **Okun's Law** seeks to describe this relationship. It may be summarized by stating each percentage drop in the unemployment rate results in a disproportionate rise in real GDP for the period measured. This observation made by Okun is based on observable empirical evidence rather than on extensive economic research and econometrics. The generally accepted ratio of Okun's Law is that for every one percent of increased employment there is a corresponding increase in real GDPof two to four percent. The significance of Okun's Law is the importance of increased employment in generating national wealth. It is often used to support economic policy which seeks to reduce unemployment and thus boost real GDP.

Macroeconomic Models

A macroeconomic model is a simulation of the forces in a macro-economy. Such models serve primarily to better understand the relationships under different variables of such macroeconomic measurements as total production, price behavior, level of employment of available resources, and total earned income. These models are used to set up hypothetical economic situations that test the effect of economic action on other variables in the model. Primarily used for forecasting future economic conditions, they are used in economic research at academic institutions, government agencies and institutions, and independent economic consulting groups. The first **macroeconomic models** were developed after World War II in Holland and the United States. A global macroeconomic model was conceived by economist Lawrence Klein, who was awarded the Nobel Prize in Economics for his work.

Laffer Curve

An important economic tool is called the **Laffer Curve**, which posits that governments may maximize tax revenue by setting tax rates at the apex of this curve and that any additional taxation actually reduces tax revenues. Developed by the economist **Arthur Laffer**, it is often used to justify tax-cutting policies popular with conservative and supply-side economists. The concept may be clarified by examining the extremes of zero taxation and a 100% tax rate. At zero taxation, the government receives no tax revenue at all. At 100% tax rates, the government also receives no tax revenue, because there is no economic incentive to work if all earned monies are collected as taxes. At some point between the two extremes is the tax rate that will secure the maximum revenue through tax receipts. Much of this is economic theory not proved in the real economic world. The curve will also vary from country to country due to different economic environments, which may skew the Laffer curve in unpredictable ways.

Economic Language and Reasoning

The methodology of economics is not unlike other sciences. The first step is the collection of **observed economic information** collected without bias. These observations ideally have measurable values that give a measure of worth. This information is collected and used in the creation of **economic models** illustrating relationships between economic variables. Examples of such relationships include price levels to consumption, and unemployment and national income. These models may be simple organizational tools for data or complex calculations of relationships between dynamic economic factors. Finally, taking the organized observed data and constructing a model, generation of **economic statistics** should follow. These statistics will be drawn from a simulated economy or economic situation and may measure the impact of an economic action on all other variables in the model. This will provide the basis for making informed economic decisions from information gained in the simulation.

Economic Policy

Economic policy refers to the broad planning and implementation of economic measures of the government in regulating and affecting economic activity. It includes wide areas of monetary and fiscal policy, and affects virtually every aspect of an economic system. Politics and social pressures play a major role in influencing **economic policy**. International agencies and institutions such as the World Bank may also play a part in determining economic policy. Several general areas of economic policy may be identified:

- **Fiscal policy and stance** refers to the government deficit or surplus and the methods of financing government operations.
- Policies on **taxation** include changing tax regulations, enforcing tax codes, and the methodology of tax collection.

- **Government spending** for usual operations of the government and special allocations for natural disasters and war.
- Determining the amount of money in **circulation**.
- The determination of **interest rates** that fall under government control.
- **International trade policy** including tariffs, reciprocal trade arrangements, and trade treaties.
- The rules and regulations that apply to the **banking system**.

Stabilization Policy

Economic stabilization may refer to two different things which require different policy and economic action. One area of **stabilization** that is common is the smoothing out of the business cycles to avoid extremes. This type of policy goal may be attained by a combination of monetary and fiscal policy in order to minimize economic fluctuations and avoid inflation or recession. Usually, the actions implemented are counter-cyclical, balancing economic trends with a goal of a stable economy. Occasionally, an unexpected economic crisis arises which demands immediate government action. Perhaps a trauma to the banking or securities markets has caused a short-term situation that requires government intervention to ease the situation. In these cases, both the government and central bank work together to remedy the situation, sometimes with the help of international economic agencies.

Fiscal Policy

Fiscal policy is the collection of money by the government to finance operating expenses and unilateral transfer payments to its citizens. The money is also used for social services and programs to maintain and improve the infrastructure of the country. The primary means of raising funds are collecting taxes from individuals and businesses, borrowing by issuing notes and bonds, and taxing services. **Fiscal policy** can be used to prime the economy by injecting funds into the system in order to increase aggregate demand. Governments must pay interest on the bonds and bills they issue to raise funds. The maturity dates vary widely between short-term treasury bills and longer-term US bonds. Monies paid as interest are raised primarily by taxation. Total net government debt is called the **deficit** and remains an issue of controversy for economists and politicians alike. This debt should be devalued by the country's inflation rate to reflect an accurate figure.

Internal Economic Stabilizers

The economy has some built-in **stabilizers** to help smooth out the business cycles. Both tax revenue and transfer payments adjust automatically when the economy begins to contract. **Income tax revenues** fall because of a decrease in employment. **Transfer payments** increase as individuals use food stamps and other government aid programs to bolster their income. This means that net disposable income is not totally dependent on the economy's level of production, and the transfer payments allow more consumption to occur than might be anticipated. Safeguards are also built in the banking system by federal insurance programs, and the stock market operates with rules and regulations imposed to prevent another panic similar to the 1929 crash. The entire economy has become more stable as a result of government policy intended to avoid the extremes in the economic cycle.

Government Intervention in Price Levels

Governments may manipulate price levels in a number of direct and indirect ways. They can directly affect levels by imposing price ceilings or price floors, limiting the range of price fluctuations of a good or service. Rent controls are an example of **price ceilings** city governments impose on landlords in some metropolitan areas. The classic example of **price floors** is the minimum wage requirements for labor in some economies. Governments may also affect aggregate demand and supply by different policies and intervention. Keynesian economists believe the government is responsible for increasing aggregate demand in a contracting economy. Monetary theorists believe the level of economic activity is directly linked to the total supply of money in the economy and use monetary and fiscal policy to determine the increase or decrease in the money supply, and thus the level of prices. **Subsidies** are another means the government may use to artificially manipulate prices in an economy.

Aggregate Demand, Supply, and Equilibrium Output

The equilibrium level of aggregate supply and aggregate demand in macroeconomics is the **equilibrium output**. The level of prices is an important determinant of equilibrium points. **Aggregate demand** reflects the total spending of individuals, businesses, and governments, as well as the net balance of payment accounts. The price level in macroeconomics determines total spending because of its impact on interest rates, the amount of wealth in the economy, and the international trade implications in price changes. Increases in prices will push up interest rates, which usually have a dampening effect on spending. The wealth of an economy decreases as prices fall, devaluing the assets in that society. Price changes can benefit a country whose prices remain stable, while their trading partners have a general increase in prices. Goods and services become cheaper to buy in the country with falling prices than in those with a stable price level. All of these factors work in concert to move an economy toward **equilibrium**.

Income Distribution and Social Welfare

Income distribution in an economy measures the patterns of the allocation of income among individuals and groups. In a sense, the **distribution of income** not only shows the income levels of individuals but also weights their relative importance in an economy. To calculate the aggregate satisfaction of the economy as a whole, the utility of each member must be measured. Any measure has subjective elements that cannot be mathematically represented in a welfare economics analysis. Such a utility-based measure treats everyone the same; there is no relative difference between a wealthy individual and a poor one. Only the satisfaction of each is measured in absolute terms. The **Maximum-Minimum function** argues that when the members of society who have the least wealth have the most relative welfare satisfaction, only then is the welfare function maximized. Any welfare policy or intervention should address those in the most need. Both of the above examples are extreme positions on **social welfare theory**. In the real world, policy usually falls somewhere in between the two.

History of the Regulations of International Commerce

When international trade began to flourish under **mercantilism**, countries protected themselves with high tariffs and restrictions on what and how goods might be traded. Over time, **free trade** was recognized as the most beneficial way to promote economic well-being. This concept has been honored over the years (with some exceptions), and free trade remains the prevailing attitude in commerce between nations. In the modern economic era, treaties and agreements among countries have resulted in a more rigidly regulated international trade environment. Free trade has historically favored nations with the strongest economies, and that remains the case today. The leading countries of the free world all advocate free trade, and developing nations have recognized the advantages in expanding their markets into the global economy. The future of free trade seems bright and bodes well for a growing international business climate.

Free Trade and Trade Barriers

The exchange of goods and services across international boundaries can be termed "**free trade**" only if the traded products are untaxed and no restrictions apply. **Trade barriers** of one kind or another or tariffs make free trade impossible and are a deterrent to commerce between nations. Trade barriers may include tariffs, limited amounts of a specific product that may be exported to a country, and other laws, restrictions, taxes, or regulations limiting the unfettered commerce between countries. Free trade is also promoted by economic policies that foster the movement of both labor and capital between countries. This climate of economic cooperation is needed to ensure a working economic relationship between trading partners. Regional trade agreements or treaties often outline the rules and regulations of commerce between nations. A country cedes some of its economic independence when engaging in free trade. There are costs as well as benefits that must be assessed.

HISTORICAL PERSPECTIVE ON FREE TRADE

Historically, free trade has been an opportunity for a country to open and develop new markets to improve its economies. **Free trade** was largely unknown until the 15th century, and had grown steadily (but not without problems) over the decades. England, with a strong manufacturing economy, was a leader in advocating unfettered commerce among countries. The theory of free trade was included in the economic works of Adam Smith and David Ricardo. Free trade has been a subject of contention over the years, with different political, social, and economic systems resisting the concept. **Protectionism**, the policy of protecting economies against competitive imports, has been the main argument against free trade. Newly developing economies use protectionism to ensure the success of their budding industries. As their economies mature and grow stronger, the pressure for new markets often makes free trade an attractive option.

Chapter Quiz

Ready to see how well you retained what you just read? Scan the QR code to go directly to the chapter quiz interface for this study guide. If you're using a computer, simply visit the online resources page at **mometrix.com/resources719/apmacroeconom** and click the Chapter Quizzes link.

AP Practice Test

Want to take this practice test in an online interactive format?
Check out the online resources page, which includes interactive practice questions and much more: **mometrix.com/resources719/apmacroeconom**

1. ______ causes a society to make tradeoffs when choosing between the production of one good or service versus another good or service.

a. Economics
b. Scarcity
c. Macroeconomics
d. Microeconomics
e. Demand

2. Assume a society has a given production possibilities frontier (PPF) representing the production of cheese and butter. Which of the following would cause the PPF to move outward?

a. The invention of a new machine that makes cheese more efficiently
b. An increase in the production of butter
c. An increase in the production of cheese
d. A decrease in the production of cheese and butter
e. An increase in the production of cheese and butter

3. A society produces 10 units of Good X and 10 units of Good Y. Then, the society changes its production, increasing production of Good X to 15 units. Production of Good Y drops to 6 units. What is the opportunity cost of producing the additional 5 units of Good X?

a. 5 units of Good X
b. 15 units of Good X
c. 6 units of Good Y
d. 4 units of Good Y
e. 5 units of Good X and 4 units of Good Y

4. Which of the following will result if two nations use the theory of comparative advantage when making decisions of which goods to produce and trade?

a. Each nation will make all of their own goods
b. Both nations will specialize in the production of the same specific goods
c. Each nation will specialize in the production of different specific goods
d. Neither nation will trade with one another
e. One nation will produce all goods for the other in addition to their own goods

Refer to the following for questions 5–6:

Consider the following production possibilities for the United States and Mexico

Production in United States

Corn (bushels)	100	80	60	40	20	0
Oil (gallons)	0	20	40	60	80	100

Production in Mexico

Corn (bushels)	0	10	20	30	40	50
Oil (gallons)	25	20	15	10	5	0

5. Which of the following statements is false?

a. The United States has an absolute advantage in corn production
b. The United States has an absolute advantage in oil production
c. The United States has an absolute advantage in both corn and oil production
d. The United States has a comparative advantage in corn production
e. The United States has a comparative advantage in oil production

6. Of the following, which is the best option for the United States?

a. Produce both corn and oil and trade neither with Mexico
b. Produce both corn and oil and trade both with Mexico
c. Produce corn and trade with Mexico for oil
d. Produce oil and trade with Mexico for corn
e. Produce neither and import both corn and oil from Mexico

7. Which of the following are true of the demand curve?

I. It is normally downward sloping
II. It is normally upward sloping
III. It is influenced by the law of diminishing marginal utility
IV. It is unaffected by the law of diminishing marginal utility

a. I and III only
b. I and IV only
c. II and III only
d. II and IV only
e. IV only

8. Which of the following is NOT a part of the business cycle?

a. Expansion
b. Contraction
c. Recovery
d. Peak
e. Stagflation

9. Which of the following correctly states a part of the Circular Flow model?

I. Households provide inputs to the factor\ market
II. Businesses spend money buying from the factor market
III. Households spend money on items from the product market

a. I only
b. I and II only
c. I, II, and III
d. II and III only
e. III only

10. Which of the following best defines American GDP?

a. The value, in American dollars, of all goods and services produced within American borders during one calendar year
b. The value, in American dollars, of all goods and services produced by American companies during one calendar year
c. The total value, in American dollars, of all American household incomes during one calendar year
d. The value, in American dollars, of a "market basket" of goods and services in one year divided by the value of the same market basket in a previous year multiplied by 100
e. The net value, in American dollars, of exports minus imports of the United States.

11. The value of a "market basket" of goods and services in one year compared to the value of the same goods and services in another year is known as what?

a. CPI
b. GDP
c. GNP
d. CCI
e. DJI

12. Which of the following is a part, or component, of GDP?

a. GNP
b. Consumption
c. Supply
d. Demand
e. Elasticity of Demand

13. What must nominal GDP be multiplied by to arrive at real GDP?

a. GNP
b. CPI
c. Supply
d. Demand
e. A price deflator

14. Which of the following would be included in GDP?

a. The value of illegal drugs sold in a nation
b. Aluminum used to make airplanes
c. Lawn care provided by a professional nursery service
d. Computer chips used in Apple computers
e. Plastic used to make product packaging

15. Which of the following could best be used in order to determine the "price deflator" for converting nominal GDP to real GDP?

a. Consumer Price Index
b. Gross National Product
c. Business Cycle
d. Phillips Curve
e. Laffer Curve

16. In which of the following circumstances does the party in question benefit from inflation?

a. A consumer buys a finished good
b. A producer buys a factor (input)
c. A person takes out a loan at a fixed interest rate
d. A company gives out a loan at a fixed interest rate
e. An investor's returns are less than the rate of inflation

17. Ivy loses her job because her skills as a seamstress are no longer required due to a new piece of machinery that does the work of a seamstress more quickly and for less money. Which type of unemployment is this?

a. Frictional
b. Structural
c. Cyclical
d. Careless
e. Technological

18. Which of the following is included in the unemployment rate typically followed by economists?

I. Structural unemployment
II. Frictional unemployment
III. Cyclical unemployment

a. I only
b. II only
c. III only
d. I and II only
e. I, II, and III

19. Which is considered part of the natural rate of unemployment?

I. Structural unemployment
II. Frictional unemployment
III. Cyclical unemployment

a. I only
b. II only
c. III only
d. I and II only
e. I, II, and III

20. Which of the following would not increase aggregate demand (AD)?

a. Government spending increases, while taxes stay the same
b. Consumer confidence about the economy grows
c. US government cuts defense spending dramatically while holding domestic spending steady
d. The US government cuts taxes
e. Business leaders feel economy is going to experience robust growth

21. The government increases spending by $1,000,000 and the multiplier is 5. How does this affect aggregate demand (AD)?

a. It has no effect
b. AD will increase by $5,000,000
c. AD will increase by $200,000
d. AD will decrease by $5,000,000
e. It is impossible to predict the effect

22. Assume that aggregate demand is at AD_1 and the government borrows money and then spends that money in order to attempt to move aggregate demand to AD_3. According to the theory of "crowding out," where is AD likely to wind up?

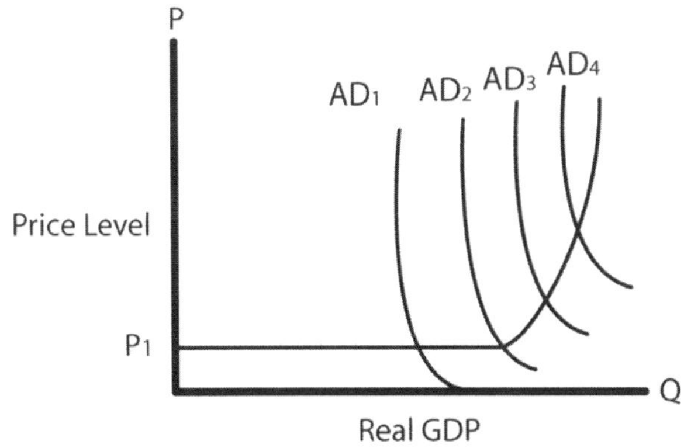

a. AD_1
b. AD_2
c. AD_3
d. AD_4
e. P_1

23. Which of the following would not cause aggregate supply (AS) to change?

a. An increase or decrease in land availability
b. The labor force suddenly increases dramatically
c. A new oil discovery causes dramatic decreases in power production
d. Worker productivity remains the same
e. A global pandemic keeps workers at home

24. How does unionized labor in an industry typically affect the wages of workers in that industry during a downturn in the economy when AD decreases?

a. It makes wages more likely to decrease
b. It makes wages more "sticky"
c. It has no effect on wages; instead, it causes AS to decrease
d. It has no effect on wages; instead, it causes AS to increase
e. It makes wages more likely to increase

25. The price of oil drops dramatically, saving soda pop manufacturers great amounts of money spent on making soda pop and delivering their product to market. Prices for soda pop, however, stay the same. This is an example of what?

a. Sticky prices
b. Sticky wages
c. The multiplier effect
d. Aggregate expenditure
e. Circular flow

26. Which of the following statements about the long run aggregate supply (LRAS) curve is correct?

a. The horizontal part represents high levels of unemployment
b. The curved part represents high levels of unemployment
c. The vertical part represents high levels of unemployment
d. The LRAS curve is a straight, vertical line
e. The LRAS curve is a straight, horizontal line

27. Assume that aggregate demand (AD) decreases. How will this decrease affect real GDP if there is a lot of unemployment as opposed to full employment?

a. If there is a lot of unemployment, prices will rise dramatically
b. If there is a lot of unemployment, GDP will stay the same
c. If there is full employment, GDP will increase dramatically
d. If there is full employment, prices will stay the same
e. If there is a lot of unemployment, GDP will decrease

28. The price of gasoline skyrockets, dramatically affecting the amount that producers spend to send their goods to market. What do you expect to happen in the short run?

a. Prices increase, GDP increases
b. Prices decrease, GDP decreases
c. Prices increase, GDP decreases
d. Prices decrease, GDP increases
e. Prices stay the same, GDP stays the same

29. AD increases, leading to an increase in price levels. At the same time, GDP and unemployment stay the same. Where does the AD curve intersect the AS curve?

a. They do not intersect
b. In the horizontal section
c. In the curved section
d. In the vertical section
e. It's impossible to say with the information given

30. Which of the following is a supply shock NOT likely to produce?

a. An increase in input prices
b. An increase in price levels
c. An increase in employment
d. A decrease in GDP
e. None of the above

31. Which of the following is correctly defined as the total of all currency, demand deposits, money market funds, saving accounts, and CDs under $100,000?

a. M0
b. M1
c. M2
d. M3
e. M4

32. Assume that the FOMC purchases bonds. Which of the following will happen?

a. The money supply increases, bond yields decline, bond interest rates decline
b. The money supply increases, bond yields increase, bond interest rates decline
c. The money supply increases, bond yields decline, bond interest rates increase
d. The money supply increases, bond yields increase, bond interest rates increase
e. The money supply declines, bond yields increase, bond interest rates increase

33. Which of the following is not always true of money?

a. It is a medium of exchange
b. It is a unit of account
c. It is a store of value
d. It is created by a central bank
e. It carries intrinsic value

34. Which of the following statements is true of money?

I. It is necessary for trade
II. It is used in trade
III. It can make trade easier

a. I only
b. II only
c. III only
d. I and II only
e. II and III only

35. How do banks create money?

a. By printing it
b. By taking it out of the Federal Reserve
c. By loaning it out
d. By putting it into the Federal Reserve
e. By taking out loans

36. Where are banks required to keep their reserves?

a. They are not required to keep their reserves
b. In their own vaults
c. With the Federal Reserve
d. With the Federal Open Market Committee
e. In the money market

37. Sally's grandmother has kept $100,000 in a cookie jar for years and then gave it to Sally, who immediately puts it in her bank in a savings account. The bank has a 20% reserve rate. Which of the following is true?

I. Excess reserves increase by $80,000
II. The money supply increases by as much as $120,000
III. Sally's grandmother earned money through inflation while she had the cash

a. I only
b. II only
c. I and II
d. III
e. I, II, and III

38. Which of the following would cause an increased demand for money?

a. A decrease in the interest rate
b. A decrease in consumer spending demand
c. A decrease in overseas demand for domestic goods (exports)
d. A decrease in uncertainty about future expectations
e. An increase in supply of goods

39. Which of the following correctly states the equation of exchange?

a. $MV = PQ$
b. $MP \times VQ$
c. MP/VQ
d. $VP = MQ$
e. $1/MP = VQ$

40. What is the money multiplier if the reserve requirement is 10%?

a. 0.1
b. 0.01
c. 1
d. 10
e. 100

41. Which of the following is true about Investment demand (Id)?

I. The Id curve is downward sloping
II. As interest rates increase, the amount of money demanded decreases
III. When interest rates are high, fewer people are willing to borrow funds for investment

a. I only
b. II only
c. III only
d. I, II, and III
e. I and III only

42. Assume that the loanable funds market is at equilibrium at the intersection of Id_{m1} and S. Then, the US government raises taxes on corporations. At which point is equilibrium established?

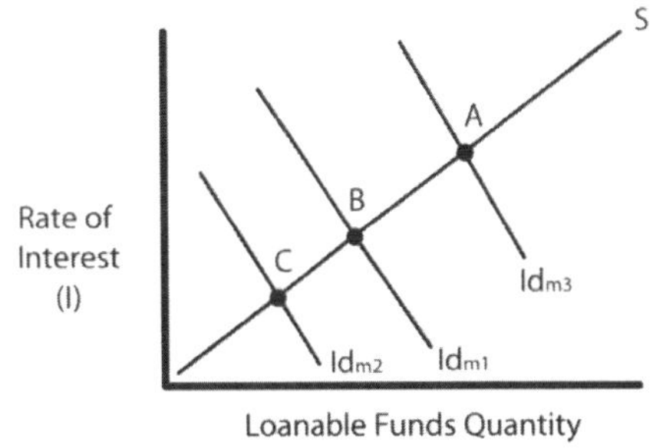

a. A
b. B
c. C
d. Some point above S
e. Between points A and B

43. Which of the following is a power of the Federal Reserve?

I. Establishing the reserve ratio requirement for banks
II. Buy and sell Treasury Bills
III. Set the Federal Funds Target Rate (the rate banks are charged to borrow from another bank's reserves) and the Discount Rate (the rate the Fed charges banks to borrow from the Fed)

a. I only
b. II only
c. I and II only
d. II and III only
e. I, II, and III

44. The Fed might do all of the following during a period with a lot of inflation except:

a. Sell Treasury Bills on the bond market
b. Increase the Federal Funds Target Rate
c. Increase the Discount Rate
d. Attempt to shift the AD curve left
e. Lower interest rates

45. According to the quantity theory of money and the equation of exchange, what would happen to the inflation rate if V and Q were constant and the money supply increased by 5%?

a. The rate of inflation would increase by more than 5% over the same period of time
b. The rate of inflation would increase by 5% over the same period of time
c. The rate of inflation would increase by less than 5% over the same period of time
d. Inflation would not be affected
e. It's impossible to determine what would happen to inflation

46. A business takes out a one-year loan to pay for an investment on January 1. On December 31 of that year they pay the loan back. During that time, the nation experiences a recession, and the overall price level in the economy drops. Which of the following statements is true?

a. The nominal interest rate of the loan is greater than the real interest rate
b. The real interest rate of the loan is greater than the nominal interest rate
c. The nominal interest rate of the loan is greater than the nominal rate
d. The loan has a real interest rate but not a nominal rate
e. The loan has a nominal interest rate but not a real interest rate

47. During a recession, the government increases spending in an attempt to increase aggregate demand (AD). This is an example of what?

a. The business cycle
b. Fiscal policy
c. Austrian economics
d. Monetary policy
e. Hyperinflation

48. During a period of inflation, the FOMC might be expected to do what?

a. Engage in expansionary monetary policy
b. Engage in expansionary fiscal policy
c. Engage in contractionary monetary policy
d. Engage in contractionary fiscal policy
e. Increase aggregate demand (AD)

49. What might be expected to happen if the government borrows money and engages in expansionary fiscal policy that is followed by a period of "crowding out?"

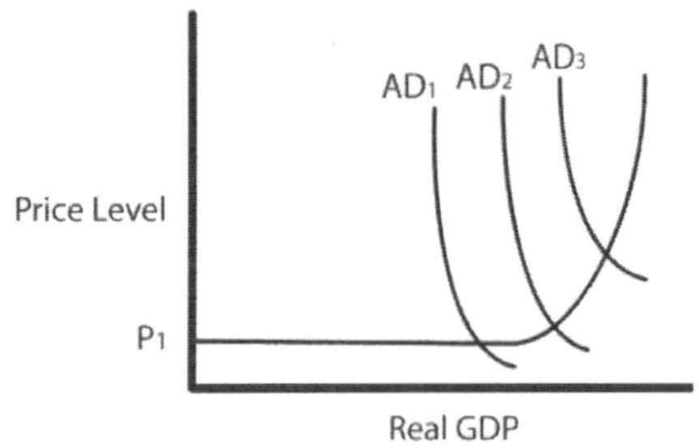

a. AD would move from AD_1 to AD_2 to AD_3
b. AD would move from AD_3 to AD_2 to AD_1
c. AD would move from AD_2 to AD_1 to AD_3
d. AD would move from AD_1 to AD_3 to AD_2
e. AD would move from AD_3 to AD_1 to AD_2

50. John Maynard Keynes advocated what?

a. Supply-side economics
b. Demand-side economics
c. Laissez faire economics
d. The Laffer Curve
e. Say's Law

51. The Laffer Curve might be used to support what?

a. Supply-side economics
b. Demand-side economics
c. An increase in government spending
d. Contractionary monetary policy by the FOMC
e. A reduction in the Discount Rate

52. Which of the following would NOT happen if the FOMC uses Treasury Bills to pursue a contractionary monetary policy?

a. The money supply decreases
b. The international value of the American dollar increases
c. The price of US goods to foreigners increases
d. American exports drop
e. Lower interest rates

53. Assume a nation's economy is in recession. The nation has an MPC of 0.9 and the government wants to enact fiscal policy to shift the AD curve by $10 billion dollars. What must the government do to its current spending rate?

a. Decrease spending by $10 billion
b. Increase spending by $10 billion
c. Decrease spending by $1 billion
d. Increase spending by $1 billion
e. Increase spending by $20 billion

54. A supply-side economist:

I. Draws inspiration from Say's Law
II. Believes that tax cuts increase tax revenues
III. Believes that tax cuts leads to shifts of the AD curve to the left

a. I only
b. II only
c. III only
d. I and II only
e. I and III only

55. Cost-push inflation might be caused by:

I. A sudden, large increase in the cost of inputs used to make products
II. Total spending exceeding total productivity
III. Governments engaging in fiscal policy

a. I only
b. II only
c. III only
d. I, II, and III
e. II and III only

56. Demand-pull inflation might be caused by:

I. A sudden, large increase in the cost of inputs used to make products
II. When total spending exceeds total productivity
III. Governments engaging in fiscal policy

a. I only
b. II only
c. III only
d. I, II, and III
e. Neither I, II, nor III

57. Hyperinflation is most likely to be associated with:

a. Demand-pull inflation only
b. Cost-push inflation only
c. Demand-pull inflation and cost-push inflation
d. Peak-pull inflation only
e. Cost-push inflation and peak-pull inflation

58. Inflation has what effects?

a. Harms all members of an economy
b. Helps all members of an economy
c. Harms no members of an economy
d. Helps no members of an economy
e. Harms some members of an economy, helps others

59. Which of the following is most likely to benefit from inflation?

a. A bond investor who owns fixed-rate bonds
b. A retired widow with no income other than fixed Social Security payments
c. A person who has taken out a fixed-rate loan
d. A local bank who has loaned money out at fixed rate
e. A person who has stored cash savings at home, not in a bank account

60. Which of the following is true of the Phillips Curve?

a. There is an indirect relationship between unemployment and inflation
b. There is an indirect relationship between aggregate supply and aggregate demand
c. There is an indirect relationship between real GDP and the consumer price index (CPI)
d. There is an indirect relationship between fiscal policy and monetary policy
e. There is an indirect relationship between the size of a contraction and the size of the expansion to follow in the business cycle

61. Which of the following would be most likely to try to combat inflation by decreasing the money supply?

a. A believer in the Laffer Curve
b. A supply-side economist
c. A Keynesian economist
d. An advocate of monetary policy
e. A believer in the Phillips Curve

62. According to the Phillips Curve, an expansionary monetary policy would do what?

I. Raise inflation
II. Decrease unemployment

a. I only
b. II only
c. I and II at the same time
d. Either I or II (but not both)
e. Neither I nor II

63. Which of the following is an element of the theory of rational expectations?

a. People have no rational reason to expect monetary and fiscal policy
b. Because people don't expect monetary and fiscal policy, they are caught unaware by it
c. Because people are caught unaware by monetary and fiscal policy, the effects of the policy are exaggerated
d. The lack of a rational reason to expect monetary and fiscal policy causes great swings from the natural rate of unemployment
e. People adjust their actions as a result of rational expectations of fiscal and monetary policy

64. Assume the Fed acts to try to keep rising prices stable. Which theory suggests that unemployment will increase as a result?

a. Phillips curve
b. Business cycle
c. Circular flow model
d. Classical economics
e. Rational expectations

65. The occurrence of which of the following argues most directly against the theory of the Phillips Curve?

I. Inflation
II. Deflation
III. Stagflation

a. I only
b. I and II only
c. I and III only
d. II and III only
e. III only

66. How is the long-run Phillips curve different than the short-run Phillips curve?

a. In the long-run Phillips curve, there is a trade-off between unemployment and inflation
b. In the long-run Phillips curve, unemployment is always greater than inflation
c. In the long-run Phillips curve, there is no trade-off between unemployment and inflation
d. In the long-run Phillips curve, unemployment equals inflation
e. In the long-run Phillips curve, there is no such thing as unemployment

Refer to the following for questions 67–68:

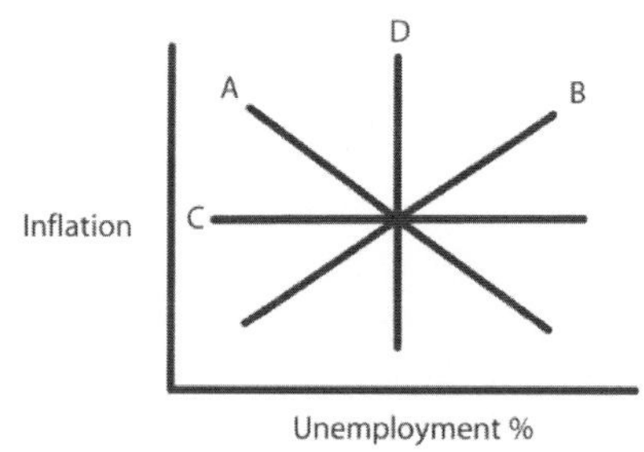

67. In the graph below, which curve (A, B, C, or D) represents the long-run Phillips curve?

a. A
b. B
c. C
d. D
e. Both A and B

68. In the graph below, which curve (A, B, C, or D) shows the NRU of the long-run Phillips Curve?

a. A
b. B
c. C
d. D
e. It is not shown

69. In economic terms, which of the following is considered investment?

a. Buying a new home computer
b. Construction of a new manufacturing plant
c. Purchase of a college education
d. Selling finished goods to a customer
e. Purchasing raw materials for regular production

70. Which of the following is not an investment in human capital?

a. A company hires new workers
b. A manufacturing plant pays to teach its workers computer skills
c. A small business gives a valued employee a raise to keep the employee with the company
d. A film studio hires a famous actress to be in a movie
e. Purchasing new uniforms for the team

71. What affect might an investment in human capital be expected to have?

a. An increase in long-run AD
b. A decrease in long-run AD
c. An increase in long-run AS
d. A decrease in long-run AS
e. A decrease in short-term AD

72. What affect might an investment in physical capital, through research and development, be expected to have?

a. An increase in long-run AD
b. A decrease in long-run AD
c. An increase in long-run AS
d. A decrease in long-run AS
e. A decrease in short-term AD

73. The value of the goods and services exported by a country within a year and the goods and services imported by that same country during the same year is captured most directly in what?

a. Balance of payments
b. Current account
c. Capital account
d. Financial account
e. Trade account

74. The value of a country's purchases of capital from other countries compared with the foreign purchases of capital within the country is most directly captured in what?

a. Balance of payments
b. Current account
c. Capital account
d. Financial account
e. Trade account

75. An increase in the value of the American dollar in foreign exchange markets might be caused by what?

a. An increase in aggregate demand (AD) in the US
b. An increase in interest rates in the US
c. A balance of payments that equals zero (debits equal credits)
d. Inflation in the US
e. A decrease in interest rates in the US

76. Country A has a current account deficit with country B. At the same time, country A has a surplus in its capital account with country B that is equal to the deficit in the current account. How would this affect the value of country A's currency in comparison with the value of country B's currency?

a. It would have no effect; the current and capital account have nothing to do with currency values
b. The value of the currency of country A would decrease in value
c. The value of the currency of country A would remain the same
d. The value of the currency of country A would increase in value
e. The value of the currency of country A would change in an unpredictable manner

77. Assume that the exchange rate between US dollars and Canadian dollars floats freely, and that American demand for Canadian dollars decreases. What is likely to happen?

a. Imports of American goods into Canada will increase
b. The price of Canadian dollars in terms of American dollars will increase
c. The price of US goods in Canadian dollars will decrease
d. The price of Canadian goods in American dollars will increase
e. The price of Canadian goods in American dollars will decrease

78. Assume that Guatemala has a surplus in its capital account. What might this mean?

a. It must also have a surplus in its current account
b. The value of Guatemalan goods bought by foreigners is greater than the value of foreign goods bought by Guatemalans
c. Its balance of payments must be unequal
d. The value of foreign goods bought by Guatemalans is greater than the value of Guatemalan goods bought by foreigners
e. The trade account is balanced

79. Assume that the value of the American dollar decreases on foreign monetary currency exchanges. Which of the following is likely to happen?

I. AS will shift right
II. AD will shift right
III. Inflation will result

a. I only
b. I and II only
c. II and III only
d. I, II, and III
e. II only

80. A country's currency increases in value on foreign currency exchange markets. What will happen as a result?

I. Exports will drop
II. Imports will rise
III. The balance of payments will rise

a. I only
b. II only
c. I and II
d. II and III
e. III only

Answer Key and Explanations

1. B: Although human wants are unlimited, the number of resources in the world available to use in order to make goods and services is limited. The limited nature of resources used to make goods and services is known as scarcity. Because resources are scarce, a society cannot make all goods and services that the people in the society want. Instead, the society must choose to use the scarce resources to make a particular mix of goods and services. Choosing to make more of one good or service forces the society to make the trade-off of making less of another good or service.

2. A: The production possibilities frontier shows the different possible combinations of goods (and/or services) a society can produce. If all other factors are even, producing more of Good A leads to a decreased production of Good B. If the PPF moves outward, that means a change in the factors of production that allows the economy to produce more goods—economic growth—has occurred. Something like innovation is an example of a cause of economic growth.

3. D: Opportunity cost is a measure of what a society gives up to produce a good (or goods). When the society decides to increase its production of Good X from 10 to 15 units, it gives up the ability to produce 4 units of Good Y (with production of Good Y dropping from 10 units to 6 units). The opportunity cost of the decision, then, is 4 units of Good Y.

4. C: When a nation follows the theory of comparative advantage, it specializes in producing the goods and services it can make at a lower opportunity cost and then engages in trade to obtain other goods.

5. D: Comparative advantage is a measure of the opportunity cost of producing a good. Mexico has an opportunity cost of only 0.5 gallons of oil for each bushel of corn produced (to increase production of corn by 10 bushels, Mexico must decrease oil production by only 5 gallons). Meanwhile, the US has an opportunity cost of 1 gallon of oil for each bushel of corn (to increase production of corn by 20 bushels, the US must decrease oil production by 20 gallons). Mexico has a lower opportunity cost for corn production, therefore.

6. D: The United States has a comparative advantage in oil production, since their opportunity cost of producing oil is 1 bushel of corn and Mexico's opportunity cost of producing oil is 2 bushels of corn. According to the theory of comparative advantage, societies (countries) should specialize in producing goods in which they have a comparative advantage and trade for other goods. Therefore, the United States should produce oil and trade for corn.

7. A: As people have more and more of something, they value it less and less. This is the law of diminishing marginal utility, and it is what causes the downward slope of the demand curve.

8. E: The business cycle includes five stages: expansion, peak, contraction, trough, and recovery. Stagflation is the name for periods when inflation and unemployment are both increasing.

9. C: The circular flow model of the economy shows, in its most basic state, how inputs, goods, and money flow through the economy's four "actors": businesses, households, the factor market, and the product market. Businesses send money to the factor market in exchange for inputs, and send finished goods and services to the product market in exchange for revenue. Households send money to the product market in exchange for goods and services, and receive money from the factor market in exchange for labor and other factors.

10. A: Answer B is a definition of gross national product (GNP), and answers C and D define other economic measures.

11. A: The Consumer Price Index is the value of a "market basket" of goods and services in one year compared to the value of the same goods and services in another year.

12. B: The following is the equation for Gross Domestic Product:

$$\text{GDP} = \text{Consumption} + \text{Investment} + \text{Government Spending} + \overbrace{(\text{Exports} - \text{Imports})}^{\text{Net Exports}}$$

13. E: Nominal GDP is the total dollar value of goods and services produced in a country in a year. However, since prices increase with inflation, nominal GDP gives a skewed view of an economy when looking at various years over time. Therefore, economists multiply nominal GDP by a price deflator that accounts for inflation in order to arrive at real GDP.

14. C: GDP measures only the value of final goods and services provided in a nation. The value of inputs—such as aluminum or computer chips—is not included, nor is the value of illegally sold goods and services such as illicit drugs.

15. A: Converting nominal GDP to real GDP requires some measure of the change in prices of goods and services within a nation over time. One could use the Consumer Price Index—the value of a fixed "market basket" of goods and services on a yearly basis—to determine the rate of inflation and then adjust nominal GDP to real GDP.

16. C: When a person takes out a loan at a fixed interest rate, and then the society experiences inflation, the inflation effectively reduces or wipes out the interest paid. For example, if a person takes out a loan at 5 percent interest, and during that time the inflation rate is 5 percent, the person has essentially taken out an interest-free loan. In the other circumstances listed, the people do feel a cost from inflation.

17. B: Structural unemployment is unemployment that results from a mismatch of job skills or location. In this case, Ivy's job skill—her ability to work as a seamstress—is no longer desired by employers. Frictional and cyclical are other forms of unemployment; economists do not use the term careless unemployment.

18. C: Economists are interested in unemployment caused by changes in the business cycle. That is what cyclical unemployment measures. There will always be some measure of structural and frictional unemployment, and those are not typically considered when assessing the unemployment picture in a nation.

19. D: It is believed that some level of frictional and structural unemployment will always exist, and that the best economists (and politicians) can hope for is to reduce cyclical unemployment to zero. Therefore, frictional and structural unemployment are sometimes referred to as natural unemployment, meaning unemployment that naturally exists within an economy.

20. C: If the government cuts defense spending but does not shift that money to other spending, that will have a negative effect on AD, causing AD to decrease. All of the other options would increase AD.

21. B: The multiplier effect states that a given increase in spending, when multiplied by the multiplier, will lead to a given increase in AD. In this case, the $1,000,000 spending increase and the multiplier of 5 lead to an AD increase of $5,000,000 ($1,000,000 × 5 = $5,000,000).

22. B: According to the theory of crowding out, when the government borrows money to increase spending, this will increase the price of money, leading to a drop in investment. That drop in investment will have a negative effect on AD, and so the government injection of funds will not have its full, desired effect (AD_3), instead winding up at AD_2.

23. D: A change in productivity, such as workers becoming more or less productive, would affect how many goods can be supplied. No change in worker productivity would cause no change in AS. Choices A, B, and C would all affect input prices and therefore would all affect AS.

24. B: When AD for the goods produced by an industry decreases, one might expect the wages paid to workers in that industry to decrease as a result. However, because unions negotiate contracts with employers, wages of unionized workers tend not to fall in these circumstances. This tendency for wages to stay the same is known as "sticky wages."

25. A: The phenomenon of "sticky prices" refers to prices that stay the same even though it seems they should change (either increasing or decreasing).

26. D: In the long run, aggregate supply does not depend on price. Aggregate supply in the long run depends strictly on the amount of capital and labor and the type of available technology.

27. E: When there is a lot of unemployment, the AS curve is horizontal. If AD decreases at this time, prices will tend to remain the same while GDP decreases. When there is full employment, the AS curve is vertical. If AD decreases at this time, prices will drop but GDP will tend to remain the same.

28. C: The increased cost of gasoline increases the cost of transportation. This is a variable cost of supply, and so the aggregate supply curve shifts inward and upward. In the short run, aggregate demand would remain fixed, leading to a rise in prices and decreased GDP.

29. D: If AD rises do not lead to an increase in GDP, the AD curve must intersect the AS curve in the vertical section of the AS curve, when employment is full. Such a situation leads to extremes of inflation.

30. C: A supply shock is caused when there is a dramatic increase in input prices. This causes an increase in price levels and decreases in employment and GDP. A supply shock causes the AS curve to move to the left (in).

31. B: There are several different measures of the national money supply; these include M1, M2, and M3; there is no M4. M1 is defined as the total of all currency, demand deposits, money market funds, saving accounts, and CDs under $100,000.

32. D: When the FOMC purchases bonds, that brings an increase to the money supply, and there is an increase in bond yields and bond interest rates. When the FOMC sells bonds, that decreases the money supply, and bond yields and bond interest rates go down.

33. E: Money, which can be created by the central bank, is defined as a medium of exchange, a unit of account, a store of value, and sometimes, a standard of deferred payment. It does not carry intrinsic value, for example, the paper used to make a one hundred dollar bill is not worth one hundred dollars.

34. E: Money can be used in trade and can make trade easier, but it is not necessary for trade, as people can barter for goods and services.

35. C: Banks create money by giving out loans. For example, assume a person puts $100 into a bank. The bank will keep a percentage of that money in reserves because of the reserve requirement. If the reserve requirement is 10% then the bank will put $10 in reserves and then loan out $90 of it to a second person. The money total, which started at $100, now includes the original $100 plus the $90, or a total of $190. The bank creates $90 by loaning it.

36. C: Banks are required to keep a particular percentage of their money on deposit with the Federal Reserve. These are deposits that the banks cannot lend. These requirements affect the bank's ability to create money (affecting the total amount a bank can loan) and are part of the Fed's toolkit for monetary policy.

37. A: Excess reserves will increase by $80,000, as the bank must keep 20% of the deposit, or $20,000, leaving $80,000. The money multiplier is 1/Reserve ratio, or 5, and that means the money supply could increase a total of $100,000 + (5 × $80,000) = $500,000. Because the cash was not able to earn interest, the cash decreased in value while it was stored in the jar.

38. A: A decrease in the interest rate would increase demand for money, as more people want to get out of investments. The other items listed would cause a decrease in demand for money.

39. A: The equation of exchange is MV = PQ. This means that M (a measure of the supply of money) multiplied by V (the velocity of money, or the average number of times a typical dollar is spent on final goods and services a year) is equal to P (the average price level of final goods and services in GDP) multiplied by Q (real output, or the quantity of goods and services in GDP).

40. D: To determine the money multiplier, use the formula MM (money multiplier) = 1/Reserve Ratio (RR). In this case, that's MM = 1/(1/10), or 10.

41. D: All three statements are different ways to saying the same thing—when interest rates for investment are high, few people want to take out loans.

42. C: When the government increases taxes on corporations, it lowers their willingness to invest—represented by the Id curve. That means that the Idm1 curve will move to Idm2, with a new equilibrium of C.

43. E: The Fed's ability to set the reserve ratio requirement for banks is the foundation of fractional reserve banking. The Fed's ability to buy and sell Treasury Bills in the bond market, called monetary policy, is the Fed's most effective way to affect the money supply. And the Fed can establish both the Federal Funds Target Rate and the Discount Rate.

44. E: During a period of inflation, the Fed's goal would be to slow down the economy. To do this, it would sell Treasury Bills on the bond market to remove money from the economy (option A), and increase the Federal Funds Rate and Discount Rate to make it harder for money to change hands (options B and C). These actions would serve to shift the AD curve to the left (option D).

45. B: If V and Q are constant, any change to P must equal any change to M, meaning that the rate of inflation would equal the growth of the money supply.

46. A: The nominal interest rate is stated interest rate, while the real interest rate is the nominal interest rate adjusted for inflation. If prices decrease during the period of the loan, the real interest rate will be less than the nominal interest rate.

47. B: When a government spends money or collects revenues (in the form taxes) in an attempt to influence the economy's performance, it is known as fiscal policy.

48. C: The Federal Open Market Committee (FOMC), part of the Federal Reserve, only has the ability to perform monetary policy, not fiscal policy. Monetary policy affects the supply of money in the economy when the FOMC buys or sells Treasury bills or changes interest rates. In a period of high inflation, the FOMC might try to counter this by reducing the supply of money. This would be an example of contractionary monetary policy.

49. D: If the government engages in expansionary fiscal policy, aggregate demand would rise. The government would have to borrow money, however, to increase its spending. This would raise interest rates, which might cause businesses to invest more, leading to a resulting decrease in AD. This is best captured by the movement of AD from AD_1 to AD_3 to AD_2.

50. B: John Maynard Keynes argued that government could help revitalize a recessionary economy by increasing government spending and therefore increasing aggregate demand. This is known as demand-side economics.

51. A: The Laffer Curve, a theoretical construction, shows the relationship between government tax rates and total government revenue, and claims that as government tax rates increase after a certain point, total tax revenues decrease. Supply-side economists sometimes use the Laffer Curve to argue against classical Keynesian demand-side economics, arguing instead for lower tax rates. They argue that increased spending by businesses will lead to increased welfare, and that supply will create its own demand.

52. E: When the FOMC sells bonds, they raise interest rates. This draws money out of the American economy, and attracts foreign investors. This causes the value of the American dollar to rise overseas, which makes American goods more expensive to overseas buyers and causes American exports to drop.

53. D: Because the MPC is 0.9, the multiplier is 10 (1/0.1). Therefore, to attain an increase of $10 billion in AD, the government must increase spending by $1 billion ($1 billion × 10 = $10 billion).

54. D: Supply-side economists believe that supply creates demand. This is Say's Law. They also believe that tax cuts increase tax revenue. This is illustrated in the Laffer Curve. Finally, they believe that tax cuts will lead to a rightward shift of the AD curve.

55. A: Cost-push inflation is caused when the price of a resource rises dramatically and unexpectedly. This is sometimes known as a "supply shock." A classic example is the supply shock experienced in the US during the 1970s when the price of oil dramatically increased.

56. B: Demand-pull inflation is caused when spending exceeds production. The "excess" demand drives up prices of goods.

57. A: Demand-pull inflation is caused when total spending is in excess of total production. This causes price levels to rise and can lead to hyperinflation.

58. E: While rising prices may hurt many members of an economy, those same rising prices may benefit other members of the same economy. For example, rising prices may help those who sell goods and services and are able to keep their costs of production low, increasing their profit margin. Meanwhile, rising prices can hurt consumers because their income is now able to purchase fewer goods and services than before.

59. C: A person who has taken out a fixed-rate loan can benefit from inflation by paying back the loan with dollars that are less valuable than they were when the loan was taken out. In the other examples, inflation harms the individual or entity.

60. A: According to the Phillips Curve, as stated by British economist A.W. Phillips in 1958, inflation and unemployment have an inverse relationship, meaning one is high when the other is low, and vice versa.

61. D: Monetary policy is the practice of shrinking and growing the money supply in order to combat inflation or deflation and otherwise attempt to "adjust" the economy.

62. C: The Phillips curve states that there is an inverse relationship between inflation and unemployment. An expansionary monetary policy would cause inflation to rise. According to the Phillips Curve, then, this increase in inflation would be joined by a decrease in unemployment.

63. E: According to the theory of rational expectations, people adjust their actions as a result of rational expectations of fiscal and monetary policy. The adjusted actions reduce the effects of the fiscal or monetary policy, and move the economy toward a natural rate of unemployment.

64. A: The Phillips Curve says that inflation and unemployment have an indirect relationship. If the Fed acts to stop inflation, then according to the Phillips Curve, unemployment will increase.

65. E: According to the Phillips Curve, when inflation is high, unemployment is low, and when inflation is low, unemployment is high. In stagflation, both inflation and unemployment are high.

66. C: In the short-run Phillips curve, there is a trade-off between unemployment and inflation. There is no such trade-off in the long-run Phillips curve. According to the long-run Phillips curve, the economy tends to stay at the natural rate of unemployment, and any changes are minor variations that will self-correct.

67. D: In the long-run Phillips Curve, unemployment stays at the natural rate of unemployment (NRU). As a result, while price levels change increase and decrease, movement along the long-run Phillips Curve is only up or down.

68. D: The long-run Phillips curve is a vertical line at the natural rate of unemployment. That's because according to the long-run Phillips curve, there is no trade-off between inflation and unemployment in the long run. Instead, the economy tends to self-correct to a natural rate of unemployment.

69. B: Any expenditure that will increase a firm's future productivity is considered investment. Of the items listed, only the construction of a new plant matches the definition.

70. E: Human capital is the labor that businesses use to make products. Answer choices A, B, C, and D are all expenditures to secure human capital in order to products (good or services).

71. C: An investment in any type of capital, assuming all else stays the same, is likely to lead to an increase in long-run aggregate supply.

72. C: An investment in any type of capital, assuming all else stays the same, is likely to lead to an increase in long-run aggregate supply.

73. B: The current account is part of what makes up a country's balance of payment account. The current account records the value of exports and imports of goods and services by a country, the country's net investment income, and the country's net transfers.

74. C: The capital account is part of what makes up a country's balance of payments account. The capital account compares the amount of foreign capital bought by a country with the amount of the same country's capital bought by foreigners.

75. B: If interest rates in the US increase, foreign investors may send more money to the US. Those investors would have to first exchange their currencies for American dollars, making the American dollars more valued (scarce) and therefore increase in value.

76. C: Country A has a deficit with country B in the current account. On its own, that would tend to reduce the value of country A's currency when compared with country B. However, the current account deficit is balance out by the capital account's surplus, leaving the value of the currency unchanged.

77. E: When demand for a foreign currency drops, the value of that currency drops. This makes it cheaper to buy goods from that foreign country.

78. B: The current account is a measurement of a country's net exports. If a country has a current account surplus, the value of the goods and services it is exporting is greater than the value of the goods and services it is importing.

79. C: If the value of the American dollar decreases, American goods will be cheaper for foreign buyers, causing AD to shift right. This will lead to inflation.

80. C: If a country's currency increases in value, foreigners will have to give up more of their own currency to get the original country's currency in order to buy the original country's goods and services. This will cause a drop in exports. At the same time, it will be less expensive for people in the original country to exchange their currency for foreign currencies, causing the price of imported goods to drop and the total value of imports to rise.

How to Overcome Test Anxiety

Just the thought of taking a test is enough to make most people a little nervous. A test is an important event that can have a long-term impact on your future, so it's important to take it seriously and it's natural to feel anxious about performing well. But just because anxiety is normal, that doesn't mean that it's helpful in test taking, or that you should simply accept it as part of your life. Anxiety can have a variety of effects. These effects can be mild, like making you feel slightly nervous, or severe, like blocking your ability to focus or remember even a simple detail.

If you experience test anxiety—whether severe or mild—it's important to know how to beat it. To discover this, first you need to understand what causes test anxiety.

Causes of Test Anxiety

While we often think of anxiety as an uncontrollable emotional state, it can actually be caused by simple, practical things. One of the most common causes of test anxiety is that a person does not feel adequately prepared for their test. This feeling can be the result of many different issues such as poor study habits or lack of organization, but the most common culprit is time management. Starting to study too late, failing to organize your study time to cover all of the material, or being distracted while you study will mean that you're not well prepared for the test. This may lead to cramming the night before, which will cause you to be physically and mentally exhausted for the test. Poor time management also contributes to feelings of stress, fear, and hopelessness as you realize you are not well prepared but don't know what to do about it.

Other times, test anxiety is not related to your preparation for the test but comes from unresolved fear. This may be a past failure on a test, or poor performance on tests in general. It may come from comparing yourself to others who seem to be performing better or from the stress of living up to expectations. Anxiety may be driven by fears of the future—how failure on this test would affect your educational and career goals. These fears are often completely irrational, but they can still negatively impact your test performance.

Elements of Test Anxiety

As mentioned earlier, test anxiety is considered to be an emotional state, but it has physical and mental components as well. Sometimes you may not even realize that you are suffering from test anxiety until you notice the physical symptoms. These can include trembling hands, rapid heartbeat, sweating, nausea, and tense muscles. Extreme anxiety may lead to fainting or vomiting. Obviously, any of these symptoms can have a negative impact on testing. It is important to recognize them as soon as they begin to occur so that you can address the problem before it damages your performance.

The mental components of test anxiety include trouble focusing and inability to remember learned information. During a test, your mind is on high alert, which can help you recall information and stay focused for an extended period of time. However, anxiety interferes with your mind's natural processes, causing you to blank out, even on the questions you know well. The strain of testing during anxiety makes it difficult to stay focused, especially on a test that may take several hours. Extreme anxiety can take a huge mental toll, making it difficult not only to recall test information but even to understand the test questions or pull your thoughts together.

Effects of Test Anxiety

Test anxiety is like a disease—if left untreated, it will get progressively worse. Anxiety leads to poor performance, and this reinforces the feelings of fear and failure, which in turn lead to poor performances on subsequent tests. It can grow from a mild nervousness to a crippling condition. If allowed to progress, test anxiety can have a big impact on your schooling, and consequently on your future.

Test anxiety can spread to other parts of your life. Anxiety on tests can become anxiety in any stressful situation, and blanking on a test can turn into panicking in a job situation. But fortunately, you don't have to let anxiety rule your testing and determine your grades. There are a number of relatively simple steps you can take to move past anxiety and function normally on a test and in the rest of life.

Physical Steps for Beating Test Anxiety

While test anxiety is a serious problem, the good news is that it can be overcome. It doesn't have to control your ability to think and remember information. While it may take time, you can begin taking steps today to beat anxiety.

Just as your first hint that you may be struggling with anxiety comes from the physical symptoms, the first step to treating it is also physical. Rest is crucial for having a clear, strong mind. If you are tired, it is much easier to give in to anxiety. But if you establish good sleep habits, your body and mind will be ready to perform optimally, without the strain of exhaustion. Additionally, sleeping well helps you to retain information better, so you're more likely to recall the answers when you see the test questions.

Getting good sleep means more than going to bed on time. It's important to allow your brain time to relax. Take study breaks from time to time so it doesn't get overworked, and don't study right before bed. Take time to rest your mind before trying to rest your body, or you may find it difficult to fall asleep.

Along with sleep, other aspects of physical health are important in preparing for a test. Good nutrition is vital for good brain function. Sugary foods and drinks may give a burst of energy but this burst is followed by a crash, both physically and emotionally. Instead, fuel your body with protein and vitamin-rich foods.

Also, drink plenty of water. Dehydration can lead to headaches and exhaustion, especially if your brain is already under stress from the rigors of the test. Particularly if your test is a long one, drink water during the breaks. And if possible, take an energy-boosting snack to eat between sections.

Along with sleep and diet, a third important part of physical health is exercise. Maintaining a steady workout schedule is helpful, but even taking 5-minute study breaks to walk can help get your blood pumping faster and clear your head. Exercise also releases endorphins, which contribute to a positive feeling and can help combat test anxiety.

When you nurture your physical health, you are also contributing to your mental health. If your body is healthy, your mind is much more likely to be healthy as well. So take time to rest, nourish your body with healthy food and water, and get moving as much as possible. Taking these physical steps will make you stronger and more able to take the mental steps necessary to overcome test anxiety.

Mental Steps for Beating Test Anxiety

Working on the mental side of test anxiety can be more challenging, but as with the physical side, there are clear steps you can take to overcome it. As mentioned earlier, test anxiety often stems from lack of preparation, so the obvious solution is to prepare for the test. Effective studying may be the most important weapon you have for beating test anxiety, but you can and should employ several other mental tools to combat fear.

First, boost your confidence by reminding yourself of past success—tests or projects that you aced. If you're putting as much effort into preparing for this test as you did for those, there's no reason you should expect to fail here. Work hard to prepare; then trust your preparation.

Second, surround yourself with encouraging people. It can be helpful to find a study group, but be sure that the people you're around will encourage a positive attitude. If you spend time with others who are anxious or cynical, this will only contribute to your own anxiety. Look for others who are motivated to study hard from a desire to succeed, not from a fear of failure.

Third, reward yourself. A test is physically and mentally tiring, even without anxiety, and it can be helpful to have something to look forward to. Plan an activity following the test, regardless of the outcome, such as going to a movie or getting ice cream.

When you are taking the test, if you find yourself beginning to feel anxious, remind yourself that you know the material. Visualize successfully completing the test. Then take a few deep, relaxing breaths and return to it. Work through the questions carefully but with confidence, knowing that you are capable of succeeding.

Developing a healthy mental approach to test taking will also aid in other areas of life. Test anxiety affects more than just the actual test—it can be damaging to your mental health and even contribute to depression. It's important to beat test anxiety before it becomes a problem for more than testing.

Study Strategy

Being prepared for the test is necessary to combat anxiety, but what does being prepared look like? You may study for hours on end and still not feel prepared. What you need is a strategy for test prep. The next few pages outline our recommended steps to help you plan out and conquer the challenge of preparation.

Step 1: Scope Out the Test

Learn everything you can about the format (multiple choice, essay, etc.) and what will be on the test. Gather any study materials, course outlines, or sample exams that may be available. Not only will this help you to prepare, but knowing what to expect can help to alleviate test anxiety.

Step 2: Map Out the Material

Look through the textbook or study guide and make note of how many chapters or sections it has. Then divide these over the time you have. For example, if a book has 15 chapters and you have five days to study, you need to cover three chapters each day. Even better, if you have the time, leave an extra day at the end for overall review after you have gone through the material in depth.

If time is limited, you may need to prioritize the material. Look through it and make note of which sections you think you already have a good grasp on, and which need review. While you are studying, skim quickly through the familiar sections and take more time on the challenging parts.

Write out your plan so you don't get lost as you go. Having a written plan also helps you feel more in control of the study, so anxiety is less likely to arise from feeling overwhelmed at the amount to cover.

Step 3: Gather Your Tools

Decide what study method works best for you. Do you prefer to highlight in the book as you study and then go back over the highlighted portions? Or do you type out notes of the important information? Or is it helpful to make flashcards that you can carry with you? Assemble the pens, index cards, highlighters, post-it notes, and any other materials you may need so you won't be distracted by getting up to find things while you study.

If you're having a hard time retaining the information or organizing your notes, experiment with different methods. For example, try color-coding by subject with colored pens, highlighters, or post-it notes. If you learn better by hearing, try recording yourself reading your notes so you can listen while in the car, working out, or simply sitting at your desk. Ask a friend to quiz you from your flashcards, or try teaching someone the material to solidify it in your mind.

Step 4: Create Your Environment

It's important to avoid distractions while you study. This includes both the obvious distractions like visitors and the subtle distractions like an uncomfortable chair (or a too-comfortable couch that makes you want to fall asleep). Set up the best study environment possible: good lighting and a comfortable work area. If background music helps you focus, you may want to turn it on, but otherwise keep the room quiet. If you are using a computer to take notes, be sure you don't have any other windows open, especially applications like social media, games, or anything else that could distract you. Silence your phone and turn off notifications. Be sure to keep water close by so you stay hydrated while you study (but avoid unhealthy drinks and snacks).

Also, take into account the best time of day to study. Are you freshest first thing in the morning? Try to set aside some time then to work through the material. Is your mind clearer in the afternoon or evening? Schedule your study session then. Another method is to study at the same time of day that you will take the test, so that your brain gets used to working on the material at that time and will be ready to focus at test time.

Step 5: Study!

Once you have done all the study preparation, it's time to settle into the actual studying. Sit down, take a few moments to settle your mind so you can focus, and begin to follow your study plan. Don't give in to distractions or let yourself procrastinate. This is your time to prepare so you'll be ready to fearlessly approach the test. Make the most of the time and stay focused.

Of course, you don't want to burn out. If you study too long you may find that you're not retaining the information very well. Take regular study breaks. For example, taking five minutes out of every hour to walk briskly, breathing deeply and swinging your arms, can help your mind stay fresh.

As you get to the end of each chapter or section, it's a good idea to do a quick review. Remind yourself of what you learned and work on any difficult parts. When you feel that you've mastered the material, move on to the next part. At the end of your study session, briefly skim through your notes again.

But while review is helpful, cramming last minute is NOT. If at all possible, work ahead so that you won't need to fit all your study into the last day. Cramming overloads your brain with more information than it can process and retain, and your tired mind may struggle to recall even previously learned information when it is overwhelmed with last-minute study. Also, the urgent nature of cramming and the stress placed on your brain contribute to anxiety. You'll be more likely to go to the test feeling unprepared and having trouble thinking clearly.

So don't cram, and don't stay up late before the test, even just to review your notes at a leisurely pace. Your brain needs rest more than it needs to go over the information again. In fact, plan to finish your studies by noon or early afternoon the day before the test. Give your brain the rest of the day to relax or focus on other things, and get a good night's sleep. Then you will be fresh for the test and better able to recall what you've studied.

Step 6: Take a Practice Test

Many courses offer sample tests, either online or in the study materials. This is an excellent resource to check whether you have mastered the material, as well as to prepare for the test format and environment.

Check the test format ahead of time: the number of questions, the type (multiple choice, free response, etc.), and the time limit. Then create a plan for working through them. For example, if you have 30 minutes to take a 60-question test, your limit is 30 seconds per question. Spend less time on the questions you know well so that you can take more time on the difficult ones.

If you have time to take several practice tests, take the first one open book, with no time limit. Work through the questions at your own pace and make sure you fully understand them. Gradually work up to taking a test under test conditions: sit at a desk with all study materials put away and set a timer. Pace yourself to make sure you finish the test with time to spare and go back to check your answers if you have time.

After each test, check your answers. On the questions you missed, be sure you understand why you missed them. Did you misread the question (tests can use tricky wording)? Did you forget the information? Or was it something you hadn't learned? Go back and study any shaky areas that the practice tests reveal.

Taking these tests not only helps with your grade, but also aids in combating test anxiety. If you're already used to the test conditions, you're less likely to worry about it, and working through tests until you're scoring well gives you a confidence boost. Go through the practice tests until you feel comfortable, and then you can go into the test knowing that you're ready for it.

Test Tips

On test day, you should be confident, knowing that you've prepared well and are ready to answer the questions. But aside from preparation, there are several test day strategies you can employ to maximize your performance.

First, as stated before, get a good night's sleep the night before the test (and for several nights before that, if possible). Go into the test with a fresh, alert mind rather than staying up late to study.

Try not to change too much about your normal routine on the day of the test. It's important to eat a nutritious breakfast, but if you normally don't eat breakfast at all, consider eating just a protein bar. If you're a coffee drinker, go ahead and have your normal coffee. Just make sure you time it so that the caffeine doesn't wear off right in the middle of your test. Avoid sugary beverages, and drink enough water to stay hydrated but not so much that you need a restroom break 10 minutes into the test. If your test isn't first thing in the morning, consider going for a walk or doing a light workout before the test to get your blood flowing.

Allow yourself enough time to get ready, and leave for the test with plenty of time to spare so you won't have the anxiety of scrambling to arrive in time. Another reason to be early is to select a good seat. It's helpful to sit away from doors and windows, which can be distracting. Find a good seat, get out your supplies, and settle your mind before the test begins.

When the test begins, start by going over the instructions carefully, even if you already know what to expect. Make sure you avoid any careless mistakes by following the directions.

Then begin working through the questions, pacing yourself as you've practiced. If you're not sure on an answer, don't spend too much time on it, and don't let it shake your confidence. Either skip it and come back later, or eliminate as many wrong answers as possible and guess among the remaining ones. Don't dwell on these questions as you continue—put them out of your mind and focus on what lies ahead.

Be sure to read all of the answer choices, even if you're sure the first one is the right answer. Sometimes you'll find a better one if you keep reading. But don't second-guess yourself if you do immediately know the answer. Your gut instinct is usually right. Don't let test anxiety rob you of the information you know.

If you have time at the end of the test (and if the test format allows), go back and review your answers. Be cautious about changing any, since your first instinct tends to be correct, but make sure you didn't misread any of the questions or accidentally mark the wrong answer choice. Look over any you skipped and make an educated guess.

At the end, leave the test feeling confident. You've done your best, so don't waste time worrying about your performance or wishing you could change anything. Instead, celebrate the successful completion of this test. And finally, use this test to learn how to deal with anxiety even better next time.

Review Video: Test Anxiety
Visit mometrix.com/academy and enter code: 100340

Important Qualification

Not all anxiety is created equal. If your test anxiety is causing major issues in your life beyond the classroom or testing center, or if you are experiencing troubling physical symptoms related to your anxiety, it may be a sign of a serious physiological or psychological condition. If this sounds like your situation, we strongly encourage you to seek professional help.

Online Resources

Due to our efforts to try to keep this book to a manageable length, we've created a link that will give you access to all of your online resources:

mometrix.com/resources719/apmacroeconom

It's Your Moment, Let's Celebrate It!

Share your story @mometrixtestpreparation